The Nature of Living Tradition

— Distinctive Features of Indian Parampara —

The Nature of Living Tradition

Distinctive Features of Indian Parampara

The Nature of Living Tradition

— Distinctive Features of Indian Parampara —

Edited by
Baidyanath Saraswati

Indira Gandhi National Centre for the Arts
New Delhi - 110 001

D.K. Printworld (P) Ltd.
New Delhi - 110 015

Cataloging in Publication Data — DK

The nature of living tradition: distinctive features of Indian parampara / edited by Baidyanath Saraswati.
Includes bibliographical references.

1. India — Civilization. 2. India — Social life and customs. I. Saraswati, Baidyanath, 1932 -

ISBN 81-246-0177-1

First Published in India in 2001

Publishers

Indira Gandhi National Centre for the Arts
Central Vista Mess, Janapath, New Delhi - 110 001

D.K. Printworld (P) Ltd.
Regd. office : '*Sri Kunj*', F-52, Bali Nagar, New Delhi - 110 015
Phones : (011) 545-3975; 546-6019; *Fax* : (011) 546-5926
E-mail: dkprint@4mis.com

Printed by: D.K. Printworld (P) Ltd., New Delhi

Contents

Introduction

PRE-COLONIAL India was secure in its foundation and mature in its thought, yet wide open for intellectual adventure – knowing and knowledge. Colonising invaders came not as conqueror but as replacement for culture and contemplative scholarship. Post-Independence India is in the process of re-visioning the primal source of culture. This prompted the Indira Gandhi National Centre for the Arts to assemble a group of knowledgeable experts to reflect upon the impact of modern Western thought on India's intellectual life and culture. A three-day national seminar on "Parampara and the Individual" was convened from 21 to 23 January 1998. The ideas discussed in this seminar must be considered by any standard to be deeply philosophical, yet they show more clearly in the anthropological realm. The proceedings of the seminar comprise this volume.

Askable Questions

The Sanskrit word *parampara* signifies layers of precipitated matter accumulated in time, as if in flood. The English word 'tradition' from Latin *tradere*, means 'to hand on', 'deliver'. The word 'individual' is derived from the Latin root *dividuus*, meaning 'able to be divided into parts or fragments', and related to the Latin *invidia*, 'had feeling or envy'.

There are questions concerning the meaning and mystery of *parampara*: What is the source of *parampara*? How is it transmitted? Is it a knowledge system? Does it hold in potential the characteristics of all orders of knowledge? A code may be? Who was the parent of its primeval seed? What lends it a sustainable identity? Do non-humans have *parampara*?

And now the question about tradition: What is tradition? Can history discover a complete tradition? Is tradition incorruptible in its form and principle? Has it a place for revelation? Is it limited to this world? How does it bridge the 'time past' and the 'time present'? What is the basis for determining chronological milestones in a tradition?

In modern parlance, *parampara* and tradition are accepted as synonyms. The key questions are: Do *parampara* and tradition read the same concept and lead the same path that measures culture? Or, do they invent their meaning and impose them on culture? Do they ascribe the individual the same place in social structure, human organisation of life?

How about tradition and modernity? Who builds them up? Do they spell two alternative world-views? Can one say that an African, an Indian or a Chinese is 'traditional' and a European 'modern'? Do they differ at the level of human sensitivity and rationality? Or, can they be placed in a single category of thought? Is the notion of modernity compatible with non-Western cultures? Is it a lifestyle or a concept reserved for a 'modern' educated elite?

The 'individual' is both creator and transmitter of *parampara* and tradition. Logically, the next set of questions are: Is the individual a passive transmitter or an active participator? How does the individual sustain the flow of *parampara* and tradition? Is it through assertion or negation of individuality, personality and subjectivity? Is the individual (especially the artist) capable of wholesome creativity, sustaining continuity, and initiating change? Does he have to take the path of a confrontation with a vaguely defined notion of *parampara* and tradition? To what extent is any human being an artist in so far as he is both active participator and observer? How does the person transcend the small 'I' into the 'We' of ever-expanding oceanic circles of consciousness? What is that experience of the 'Self' where duality between 'subject' and 'object' is lost? How does the individual artist become empowered to transmit in part or whole the residual quintessence of *parampara* in ever renewing forms of contemporary relevance? What is the source of creativity and innovative urge which enables a person to be contemporary and yet to be a link in the transmission? Is conflict inevitable?

Parampara and Primordial Pattern

By *parampara* we mean 'a nearly self-sufficient partial modality of human manifestation ruled by *dharma* (Order)'. As an earth-bound self-organising self-same system operating within the limit of time, *parampara* is essentially related to the original divine. The possible modalities (forms) of *parampara* cannot be counted, but there is a transcendent unity of the different forms originating in course of time. Truly speaking, the mystery of *parampara* is impenetrable. But the primordial pattern constituting the way of human life is repeated and replicated analogically on a variety of levels and in different modalities and forms. It is both cosmological and sociological, divine and human, universal and local. Man lives in *parampara* fully when he does not question the Supreme Principle of Life.

B.N. Saraswati presents an overview of the primordial pattern of *parampara*, as reflected in Hindu scriptures: Epistemologically, the word *parampara* refers to a 'deposit' of knowledge to be nourished and handed down to posterity. Originally, it was revealed to the ancient seers who became the First Trustees of *parampara*. Ontologically, as a self-existent primeval seed of knowledge, it is imperishable in essence. Cosmologically, it follows the universal cycle of creation — dissolution — and recreation. Dissolution follows the divine depositions. Metaphorically, it is an Inverted Tree with roots upward and branches downward. It is a Law by itself, an Order (*rita*), which both God and man uphold. As cultural marker, it makes a social group unique and autonomous. Within the expanding circle of *parampara* all cultures find their finest expression and fulfilment. By nature, *parampara* is hieratic, not hierarchical. By definition, it is changeable, but the change occurs within a given limit (*maryada*).

M.C. Joshi's contribution prepares the groundwork for understanding Buddhist *parampara*: It is difficult to establish the historicity of Buddha. The scriptures refer to primeval Buddha who was the first to preach the Law and establish the Order. The subsequent Buddhas — over a hundred humans — did *not* explore anything new, but only repeated whatever was earlier expounded and practised by the primeval Buddha. Each Buddha is said to have achieved victory over the evil deity. The concept of future Buddha as the saviour of the Order makes the integral continuity and transcendent unity possible. The notion of the five non-human *dhyani* Buddhas widens the universality of *parampara* and its transcending power, whereby historicity and ahistoricity converge and a mystery religion of peace is born.

P. Nandakumar's paper presents another modality of *parampara*: Historicity and ahistoricity come together from the life of the Vaishnava Tamilians. Enriched by strong scholastic, ritualistic and artistic pursuits, the two thousand-year old *Tiruppavai parampara* flows on majestically as a perennial, colourful, soul-sustaining river of life. Secured by successive spiritual teachers and founded on and centered in a timeless wisdom, it gains a deeper understanding of man and his universe.

P.L. Sharma's exhilarating vision enters into the depths of the musical *parampara*: Like a society, *parampara* is an abstraction. It is blending of *anadi* (beginningless) and what is ascribed to a specific individual contribution. There is a structural difference between tradition and *parampara*. Whereas tradition implies a static set of knowledge, skill and belief, *parampara* has a dynamic flow which provides room for change, innovation, and individual preference. For instance, the knowledge or skill of music is transmitted orally. In the initial stage, the student is required to imitate or reproduce whatever the teacher sings or plays, but soon one is guided towards improvisation on one's own.

R.R. Menon says: As expression or reflection, *parampara* is not a mere tradition, not a mere belief, not a word but an expression close to Nature. In the context of music what makes one a musician is not the practice of song but the cultivation of Self. It is this Self within a musician that shines out of his art and makes music divine. So, it can be said that *parampara* is concerned with the transformation of man.

S.K. Mahapatra explores the ambivalent relationship between poetic creativity and *parampara*: There is a distinction between a poet, a visual artist, and a musician facing *parampara*. The poet seeks to transcend the ambivalence by working out an upward movement for the words — from the language of commonality to that of poetry. He mediates between original and unique experience.

R.C. Shah presents a new path to interpreting *parampara*: The poet Agyeya, the leader of the modernist movement in Hindi, and T.S. Eliot, who saw the values of European culture threatened from within itself and sought an ally in Eastern *parampara*. To upgrade his tradition in the garb of *parampara*, he gained insights from Indian metaphysics and poetry. Agyeya, his counterpart, on the other hand, needed the corrective for revitalisation of the metaphysically sound but creatively almost exhausted *parampara*. The poet W.B. Yeats speaks beautifully of the 'great memory' or the 'age-long memorial self' not only of man but of bird and beast alike — because they too are the living symbols of the divine order, the *rita*. Shah the poet has chosen great poets from the secular West to demonstrate that *parampara* is a universal paradigm.

Tradition as Hiero-history

Tradition perceived as history refers to time in which every time is restored to the present. Here restoration of time is not to be understood as bringing back the original state; it means a continual renaissance. It is important to make a distinction between *parampara* and tradition. As timeless reality, *parampara* is a cosmocentric vision originating from the contemplation of the unknown cosmos (that needs to be remembered). Man must seek his freedom and fulfilment within the given limits of his life-world. Those who are unaware of the limits fall into the personalised, subjective box of modern psychology. Tradition, on the other hand, gives importance to anthropocentric vision which is concerned with handing down the organisational memory from one generation of humans to another. Its emphasis is on hiero-history of human mind and creativity, the awareness of power, knowledge and authority.

S.C. Malik's paper expands by increasing exchange between the domains of *parampara* and tradition, and considers anew the concept of tradition and modernity: Taking a holistic view, *parampara* is a movement, a continuous change in the 'now', the past and future coalescing and emerging from the experiential present, the 'now' which is not a mere abstraction of the intellect. Tradition in this sense is *not*, as social scientists believe, something that is static, something that stifles imagination and is soulless repetition lacking originality. Tradition and modernity do not refer to mutually exclusive categories, as considered by some. The unreflective use of these terms has created confusion.

M.M. Agarwal the philosopher finds *parampara* and tradition in a symbolic integration and refutes the sociological theory that tradition is static: *Parampara* signifies an ordered stream of consciousness which is directed towards the perfection — the *telos* — for whose fulfilment it exists and receives its identity. Tradition is a dynamic, intelligent human phenomenon. The accumulated wisdom of a community plays a dynamic role by providing a starting point for the younger generation. By virtue of its past success, tradition provides the necessary impetus and inspiration to move towards the *telos*.

A. Rai takes an etymological approach to tradition: The question of tradition would arise in very different forms in traditional societies. The tradition-bound people would argue about matters of details and nuances of interpretation, but the question of their particular and even elective relationship to tradition would simply not arise. In the renewed concern with the question of tradition one finds the tradition dusted and aired, refurbished, trimmed-down, tricked-out, invented, fabricated. This sense of nostalgia is reflected in modern writings.

A.R. Kelkar's paper connects up the demystification and remystification of tradition: Tradition tends to be opposed to innovation or experiment and often lapses into letting things take their course. Indian tradition for instance, is a palimpsest and has unresolved tensions built into itself. Depending on the context, *parampara* is opposed to *shastra* (conscious discipline), *deshya* (regional or local) or *adhunik* (recent/new). Tradition and modernity differ with reference to world-views and lifestyles. The world wide transition from tradition to modernity is the reality of time. While the philosophical tools of European modernity are not quite satisfactory for resolving or transcending the opposition between tradition and modernity, Indian thinkers have offered the platforms for transcending the either-or approach.

Individual as Person

The mystery of *parampara* emerges from *purusha* (person), the cosmic man, the personal aspect of the whole of reality. All things both animate and inanimate — animals of every type, liturgical formulas, the four castes of men, the cosmic powers — have their origin in *purusha*. The concept of person excludes isolation, alienation, and expresses interconnections and unity. The Veda, the root of all knowledge was revealed to the sages, the best among humans, who shared the rhythms of life and thought with the entire universe. The divine sense of individual (Soul, Self, Person) governed the early humanity. Over time, it was lost. The modern Western image of 'individual' (the exaggerated sense of individualism) is inseparably linked to materialism and consumerism. The present discourse helps the reader to understand that individual as person extends beyond individualism.

K. Malik's paper brings out an anthropological dimension of the individual: The stormy history of this dying century began with Western Europe, the one which inheriting its legacy of protestant attitudes and questioning of sacrosanct truths in the eighteenth-century spawned mobile societies of enormous plasticity to become inflexible. The new politico-social order is yet the ground for a pessimistic outlook and much bafflement. In the new order of secular modernity, the individual has come into a sharper person profile, and his intellectual and volitional powers have also enhanced. But, at the same time, a parallel conformity (or uniformity) has been imposed on him. The individual has come to be cog in a machine. The future of the individual lies in re-establishing the sacred. The sacred concerns the individual qua individual, or that part of him which can commune with his fellow beings and share sentiment, but can do so only through some non-coercive energy, i.e., through insight, sympathy, the growth of fraternal feeling and so on. The sacred cannot live too securely in company with inhuman environment.

A.R. Kelkar's essay provides a warning: Individual today — whether thinker, artist, leader, seer, saint or hero — is at the crossroads. There is no scope of embracing one and jettisoning the other.

A. Rai focuses on the connection between 'longing' and 'belonging': The identity of the individual today has gone from signalling sameness to becoming a sign of the politics of destructive difference.

M.M. Agarwal goes deep into the phenomenology of 'I': The popular ideas about individual, individuality and the consequent individualism are mistaken. The individual and the tradition are necessary to each other. The individual whose behaviour is directed simply by the inner compulsion of the cultural self has no real individuality. The real individuality lies in freedom *from* the conditioned self, not for the self. The sages set-up the spiritual tradition of the quest and opened up the landscape of infinite possibility of life for the individual. In the total understanding of life, the individual is placed squarely within the fold of the spiritual tradition. There is no salvation in the collective, nor does it lies in the greedy egoistic individualism.

S.C. Malik draws a contextual difference: There is a difference between the individuals in traditional societies and those in the spirit of the main current of modernity. The individual in traditional societies considers himself a part of an organic whole towards the harmony of which he strives. Today, individualism is taken for granted; it is ubiquitous and unquestioned.

R.C. Shah voices the inalienable worth of supra-individual:It is the awakened individual (*vyakti* literally means manifestation) which makes the self-awareness and renewal of the *parampara* possible. What constitutes the greatness or the uniqueness of an individual has nothing to do with the individual as such; it is the radiance through him of something supra-individual, mysterious or divine. The individual Self (*jivatma*) is sufficiently illumined through intuition or discipline to realise the Unity of Being which all civilisations, all religions and artistic endeavours have aspired to.

S.K. Mahapatra has also highlighted the inner power of the individual: The poet, for instance, has an extraordinary capacity for transcending the common man's language to explore the inlaid nuances of the word. The one who makes *parampara* in poetry is not an ordinary individual.

R.R. Menon holds the same view: The musical *parampara*, which originates from the individual, is concerned with the transformation of man. The one who builds *parampara* is not a common man, an ordinary individual, stamping his feet on the earth.

P.L. Sharma brings to light the importance of creative genius: The origin of musical *parampara* lies in anonymity; the contributor is an anonymous individual.

P. Nandakumar has shown that luminous individuals can be found amidst common people: Andal, the originator of the *Tiruppavai parampara*, composed soulful devotional songs in a domestic atmosphere. For the devotees, of course, she was a paradigmatic figure — Mother Lakshmi, Sita and Rukmini. She rose much above the ordinary individual.

M.C. Joshi calls attention to the phenomenon of transcending individuality: In the Buddhist *parampara*, the representation of human Buddha is an impossibility. There were many Buddhas, each contributing to the growth of *parampara*. The ever present, ever invisible and even silent Buddha nullifies the claim for an exaggerated value of individuality.

B.N. Saraswati holds that *parampara* is formed by 'abstract individuals': Because of the fusion of primordial patterns, *parampara* is continually re-born by itself. The ancient and the living merge into a single reality. Even the individual creation is not wholly determined by man. At the highest level of thought the relationship between *parampara* and the individual is inexplicable.

In conclusion, the contributions of this volume represent a wide spectrum of disciplines, none of which is closed, and no contributor is constrained by the limits of formal knowledge. The contemplation comes naturally first through experience, then reflexion through philosophies, religions and popular wisdom, subsuming many perspectives on *parampara*, person, and tradition. There has been much debate over the past few years on tradition and modernity. The issue has been raised here in a different light. The result is a lively affirmative analysis based on the intermixing of experience and knowledge. What comes out is the nature of living tradition.

Spring 2000 **Baidyanath Saraswati**

1

Parampara: A Universal Paradigm

Baidyanath Saraswati

Parampara: An Inverted Tree

THE Sanskrit word *parampara* signifies layers of precipitated matter accumulated in time, as if in flood. Epistemologically it refers to a deposit of knowledge to be nourished and to be handed down to posterity. This definition implies three operant ideas: (1) that there exists by itself a deposit of knowledge; (2) that there are depositories capable of communicating with the mind and memory of the Earth; and (3) that there are ways of deposition and structuring of reality.

1. DEPOSIT

The Ultimate Reality is of the nature of the Word Principle (*shabda-tattva*) from which are manifested all the objects and the whole cosmos. The Word, imperishable, is the Firstborn of Truth, mother of the Veda and hub of immortality (*TB*, II.8.8.5). The first creation is *mahat* (intellectual principle), the seventh the creation of human beings (*GP*, II). The Word has been measured in four degrees (*pada*), three kept closely hidden (*guha nihita*); men speak only the fourth degree of wisdom (*RV*, X.90.4). This perception guides every aspect of human life and culture.

As commonly understood, human knowledge, like all other things of the world, has multiplied in time. The deposit of knowledge consists of eighteen classes of basic texts which remain the perennial source of all kinds of learning. Of these, the Veda, the root of knowledge, was revealed to the *rishi*s, the first among men. The Vedic text is classified into *Samhita*, *Brahmana*, *Aranyaka*, and Upanishad. The *Samhita* is the collection of the revealed hymns; the

Brahmana is the human composition in prose of the ritual acts, as described in the *Samhita*; the *Aranyaka* contains explanation of rituals as a symbol of hidden Truth; and the Upanishad, the outgrowth of the *Aranyaka*, debates on the deeper meanings of the Truth. Taken together, these four classes of texts called *Shruti* (what is heard) are accepted as 'Unlimited in extent and unequalled in authority' (*Manu*, 1.3). Intellectualisation of the *Shruti* produced another class of text called *Smriti* (what is remembered), also known as *Dharmashastra*, the code dealing with the expositions of duties and the maintenance of the social fabric. The *Shruti* and the *Smriti* formed the denser inner layers of *parampara*.

From the *Brahmana*, the intellectualised ritualistic text (*karmakanda*) of the *Samhita*, grew into a class of literature called *Kalpasutra*. The *Kalpasutra*, in time, got divided into three: (1) *Shrautasutra*, which deals with the Vedic sacrifice; (2) *Grihyasutra*, which ordains domestic ceremonies; and (3) *Dharmasutras*, which considers matters concerning the civic life. The last two together are named *Smartasutra*. The epic, which includes the Purana, is also one among the *Smriti*, and treated on the same footing as *Dharmashastra*. A complete *Kalpa* covers all Laws. Re-intellectualisation of the *Shruti* and the *Smriti* gave rise to yet another class of literature called *Nibandha*, commentary. To this may well be added the immemorial customs and practices of the virtuous men, occasionally published under the rubric *shadachara* and *shishtagama*. Treasured in this deposit is another vast corpus of texts produced by the heterodox faiths such as Buddhism, Jainism and others. All these formed the weaker outlayers of *parampara*.

The *Smriti* texts claim that in their code `appears the system of Law in its full extent, with the good and bad properties of human actions, and the immemorial customs (*achara shaswata*) of the four classes of men' (*Manu*, 1.107). The orally transmitted customs and usages of the non-literate as also of women (*lokachara* or *striyachara*) form an integral part of the living spirit of culture.

2. DEPOSITORY

The primeval seed of knowledge is self-existent. It revealed itself to the ancient seers who possessed infinite wisdom and Truth. According to a *pauranika* description, Brahma created seven or nine mind-born sons (*manasputra*-s) who became the first institutors and observers of ritual. After them were born many other spiritually developed *rishi*s who nourished the primary deposit. As a class of depositories, they were the first trustees of the *Shruti-Smriti parampara*.

The later descendants of the *rishi*s subsequently divided the trust amongst themselves. The brahmanas were assigned to commit to memory one of the four Vedas (*Rig*, *Yajur*, *Sam* and *Atharva*) and to follow one of the *sutra*-s, the manuals of ritual. They were called upon to devote their entire life to learning and teaching the *shastra*. Today, even those brahmanas who no longer study the *shastra* are still identified with the Vedas. While performing a sacrament every Brahmana utters his name (not surname), the name of his primeval *rishi* ancestor (*gotra-pravara*), the Veda, the *shakha* or the branch of the Veda, and the *sutra* to which he is identified by his family *parampara*.

Similarly, the followers of the other spiritual paths, named as *sannyasi*, *vairagi*, *sadhu*, *santa*, *mahatma*, *muni* and *bhikhu*, nourish their respective *parampara*-s.

The fact that in the *sanatana parampara*, no single class of men can truly claim an exclusive right to deposition is reflected in the ancient ordinance of Manu (VIII.41) which enjoins on the king to let the people themselves legislate by enforcing (and recognising) the Law (*dharma*) of family (*kula*), caste (*jati*), class (*varna*), and country (*janapada*). Also, a certain geographical area has been marked as the authentic place of deposit. Brahmavarta (the tract of land between the two rivers Sarasvati and Drishadavati), for instance, is such a place. For, `the custom preserved by immemorial *parampara* in that country, among the four pure classes, and among those which are mixed, is called approved usage' (*Manu*, II.18).

Thus, the depositories of the *sanatana parampara* are of various classes and categories. The smallest unit is family; but even the individual practices of good men and one's own personal satisfaction (after due deliberation) have been recognised as the roots of *dharma* (*Manu*, II.6).

3. DEPOSITION

The concept of *parampara*, implying deposition of knowledge comparable to the formation of layers of precipitated matter caused by the flood, is derived from the *pauranika* descriptions of the appearance and disappearance of the primordial knowledge.

> At the end of the four Ages there is a disappearance of the Veda, and it is the province of the seven *rishi*s to come down upon Earth from Heaven to give them currency again. In every *krita* Age, Manu (of the period) is the legislator, or the author, of the body of the Law, the *Smriti*. Vishnu in the form of Kapila and other inspired teachers, assiduous for the benefit of all creatures, imparts to them true wisdom. In the *treta* Age, he restrains the wicked, in the form of universal monarch, and protects the three worlds. In the *dvapara* Age, in the person of Veda Vyasa, he divides the one Veda into four, and distributes it to innumerable branches. And at the end of *kali* or fourth Age he appears as *kali* and re-establishes the iniquitous in the path of rectitude. In this manner the universal spirit preserves, creates and at last destroys all the worlds. — *VP*, III.2

Cosmic dissolution follows re-creation. Similarly dissolution of *parampara* follows divine deposition. This process goes on and the primeval seed of knowledge (*shabda-tattva*) alone exists eternally.

The quality of deposition in each Age is of unequal merit. As has been allegorically stated, the cow of *dharma* in the *krita* Age stands on all its four legs; in the *treta* on three legs; in the *dvapara* on two legs; and in the *kali* Age it is limping on one leg alone (see *S. Bhag*, XI.3).

The process of deposition begins with divine intervention and revelation, followed by moral intellectualisation and re-intellectualisation. The scholastic process scrupulously eliminates any disconcerting element that may arise in the deposit. Each element to be deposited must withstand the criteria of Truth (*pramana*). The Veda is the *pramana*, the undisputed means of arriving at the notion of *dharma*. The *Smriti*, the product of excellent human mind, is also no less authentic a text. The *Shruti* and the *Smriti* are perceived not separately but in terms of a divine continuum.

> Whatever has been ordained for any person by Manu, that has been fully declared in the Veda, for that sage was omniscient.
>
> — *Manu*, II.7

> A learned man, after carefully scrutinising all this (*Smriti*) with the eye of knowledge, should in accordance with the authority of

> the revealed texts (*Shruti*) be intent on the performance of his duties. — *Manu*, II.8
>
> But when there are two sacred texts (*Sruti* and *Smriti*), apparently inconsistent, both are held to be Law, for both are pronounced by the wise to be valid and reconcilable. — *Manu*, II.14

It has been cautioned that the deposit must be kept in extremely good care by learned men, and transmitted duly to the deserving persons (*adhikari*). For, in it lies the welfare of the whole humanity.

> A code which must be studied with extreme care by every learned Brahman, and fully explained to his disciples, but must be taught by no other man of an inferior class. — Manu, I.103
>
> This most excellent code produces everything auspicious; this code increases understanding; this code procures fame and long life; this code leads to supreme bliss. — *Manu*, I.106
>
> Immortal custom is transcendental Law, approved by the sacred scriptures, and in the codes of divine legislators, let every man, therefore, who has a due reverence for the supreme spirit which dwells in him, diligently and constantly observe immemorial custom. — *Manu*, I.108

A curious and interesting account of the primeval human race appears in the *Markandeya Purana* (XL.10):

> Social and moral evolution of this primitive humanity has been attributed to some trees called *kalpa* which, until the beginning of the *treta* Age, were producing houses and honey (not made by bees) and providing every kind of enjoyment and subsistence, clothing and ornament to those people; but afterward, in course of time when those people grew covetous, their minds being filled with selfishness they fenced the trees (*vrikshama*), and those trees perished by reason of that wrong conduct on their part.

Whatever merit or meaning the myth of *kalpa* may have, the Tree is undoubtedly the most appropriate and excellent metaphor for describing the *sanatana parampara*.

The primeval seed of knowledge struck roots in the Veda which, having been divided into four principal stems, soon branched out into numerous *shakha*-s. The Tree of the *Shruti* developed a huge trunk; with the formation of the Smriti, its innumerable branches and leaves grew out in countless textual, oral and transcendental *parampara*-s. This Tree of *parampara* can well be demonstrated by showing genealogical connections between all the *sampradaya*-s and *pantha*-s, and of the eighteen principal classes of texts which are considered the perennial source of the entire *sanatani* scholastic *parampara*. But this great Tree has two peculiarities; first, it is an inverted tree with roots upward and branches downward; and, secondly, it flowers in its roots and not in its branches but bears fruits all over, even to this day.

Parampara: A Cultural Marker

Culture may be conceived as a depository class bearing within itself a deposit of knowledge of wide varieties, accumulated in space-time. The deposit of each culture is made up of two parts: the manifest and the unmanifest. The manifest part contains the knowledge of things divinely revealed and/or humanly discovered. The unmanifest part contains beliefs and hopes of what is yet to be revealed and/or discovered. Divine revelations and human discoveries keep the manifest part of the deposit continually in a state of flux. The unmanifest part remains in a perpetual state of mystification. In the situation, any classification of cultures based on their empirical content, that is, the manifest part of the deposit, is bound to be partial and lasting only for a time. A relatively more enduring and valid classification can be sought in terms of their modes of transmission of knowledge. There are three principal modes of transmission: oral, textual and transcendental. Adopting one of these as the *essential* mode of survival, all cultures may be grouped into three basic types, called Oral (*laukika*), Textual (*shastriya*), and Transcendental (*naivrittika*).

Oral (Laukika)

The peasant potters fall under the category of *laukika* culture. Their entire way of life is guided essentially by the verbal testimony, or the collective memory, of their elders. In their productive techniques, i.e., the knowledge of suitable clay and techniques of processing, beating, enlarging, painting, firing, and such other methods of manufacture, the potters rely *exclusively* upon oral sources. Their productive organisation also operates on oral mechanism. The price of each article is fixed without a complex cost accounting. Their economic relationship with the clients (*jajamana*) is unrecorded and yet such a contract is faithfully honoured and renewed, or carried on, from one generation to the next. In matters of social organisation, the potters again fall back upon the memory of their elders. The rules of marriage and inheritance are conventional, but strictly followed. A breach of the conventional rules is considered an offence against the whole community and hence tried in the potters' caste-council (*jatiya panchayata*) in accord with the unwritten Laws (orally transmitted *lokachara*). Their food-related taboos and domestic rituals and festivals are prescribed and conducted orally by the community elders. Their women are experts in domestic and ceremonial usage (*striyachara*); men are specialists in community rituals. The entire code of their behaviour is the unwritten *loka parampara*.

2. Textual (Shastriya)

In contrast, the *shastriya* culture is based *essentially* on the reliance in and the authority of the *shastra*. The Brahmanic culture is a *shastriya* culture, because the entire social and ritual life of the Brahmanas is guided essentially by the ancient texts. Their occupation is determined by the *Dharmashastra*. Their knowledge of the arts and aesthetics, literature, medicine, astronomy, architecture, and all such theoretical and applied learning is based primarily on textual sources. Their rules of marriage, domestic rituals, inheritance, and criminal Laws are laid down in great details in the *shastra*. Breach of the Laws are dealt with at the textual level. Necessary purificatory rights for various kinds of offences are prescribed by the *shastra*, and the person who has committed the offence is required to consult a *dharmadhikari*, specialist in the Law, for appropriate action. There is hardly anything in the life and ways of a brahmana that may escape the omnibus *shastra*.

3. Transcendental (Naivrittika)

Different from both the *laukika* and the *shastriya* is the *naivrittika* culture whose members are specialists in the cultivation of excellence in transcendental knowledge. People of the *naivrittika* culture are marked off by their disinterested worldly act (*nivratta-karma*), in contrast with those who act with the object of attaining worldly gains (*pravritta*, or *kamyakarma*). To exist in this world they have to perform necessarily all acts of subsistence. But they do it disinterestedly. Their primary concern is transcendence. They practise penance and cultivate transcendental knowledge. As a class of ascetics, they renounce the worldly life of the householder (*grihastha*). The fact that they are no longer a part of the householder-culture is demonstrated at the time of their initiation (*samnyasa samskara*) when the novitiate performs his own funeral rites. This ceremony signifies ritual death of this-worldly individual. It symbolises new birth for a spiritual life and culture. The shaving of the head at the time of initiation also mean renunciation of this-worldly life and ushering in spiritual culture. At one stage in the ceremony, the novitiate walks seven steps stark naked, which suggests that he has wiped off his worldly impurities, and then the *guru* bows down before him and gives him a new name. The preceptor's bowing down to the pupil symbolises the latter's entry into a new world or joining the fraternity of the transcendental culture in which all are *essentially* equal. For practical and historical reasons, the people of *naivrittika* culture are organised into various groups forming spiritual lineages and families. More importantly, they are graded according to their state of transcendence such as *kutichaka*, *bahudaka*, *hansa*, *paramhansa*, *turiyaleeta*, and *avadhoota*. The ascetics are culturally autonomous in the sense that the Laws of the householders do not apply to them, even though the physical survival of most of them depends on the householders.Theoretically, however, the existence of a biologically self-sustaining *naivrittika* culture cannot be truly ruled out. At least, such was the culture of the ancient *rishi*s.

This classification presents a characteristic dimension of *parampara* as a culture marker. It shows how each of the three forms of culture is shaped uniquely and autonomously according to its mode of transmission. The Oral culture is formed, preserved and transmitted by the powers of collective learning; and the Transcendental culture by the powers of self-knowing. The ultimate testimony of the latter lies in the practice (*prayoga*), in which case the Truth is revealed to a person directly and without the use of human language. Obviously, the typology does not preclude the possibility of inter-cultural communicability. But surely, in this framework, any ordering of *parampara* into high and low, great and little, is logically untenable. For, each deposit of knowledge is governed by a self-organising (self-generating and self-regulating) system which allows it to function autonomously and efficiently.

At this point in the analysis something needs to be said about *parampara* and the individual. *Parampara* is neither style nor civilization. It is an ideological system, basically a world-view, opposite to the individualistic, egalitarian, atomistic modernity. It exists in a nature-integrated culture where there is no `history' which deals with the human phenomena individualised by time, no `mechanical' thinking about human existence, no blind mechanics of the natural world, no church of materialistic progressivism, and no individual in his singular glory. It is a Law of culture formulated by `abstract individuals' and fused to primordial patterns that are continually reborn. It contains the ancient and the living spirit of culture. Through it man receives all celestial influences and develops the ability to perceive and participate in the subtle energies of authentic life.

Parampara: A Timeless Reality

Going into the depths of the inner vision, one would clearly see that *parampara* is itself by itself a Law which both God and man uphold. The seed of knowledge, in the nature of the Word-Principle, is eternally present. Only one-fourth of it is revealed to mankind. What is handed down to man is his primary *parampara* which in course of time degenerates and disappears. God in his incarnation comes down upon the Earth at the end of every age, and re-creates and re-establishes the *parampara* of man. And thus the process of *parampara*-making continues eternally. Based on the Truth-abiding principle, it passes through a five-fold consideration of (1) *patrata*, competence, (2) *pramana*, criteria of Truth, (3) *purnatva*, fullness, (4) *paristhiti*, compelling situation, and (5) *parishuddhi*, purification. Of these the first three are procreative and the last two restorative in purpose and performance.

1. PATRATA

Can one write today a new *Smriti*? The forthright answer is: 'No'. The Rishis alone could write the *Smriti*, for they were the Omniscient — one who is perfect in knowledge (*jnana*) and scrupulous in observance of righteousness (*sadachara*), but no man of inferior quality can write *shastra* (that which disciplines man). Competence (*patrata*) depends not on learning and logic but profoundly on purity of life (*sattva*) and the inner character (*antardharma*) of a person.

2. PRAMANA

In matters of usages and customs, the ancient Lawgivers (*Manu*, II.6; *Yajn*, 1.7) have declared the quadruple sources, namely, *Shruti*, *Smriti*, usage of good men, and self-satisfaction born of due deliberation. Only that work which accords with the canonical standard (*shastraman*) is the true *shastra-parampara*.

3. PURNATTVA

Fullness is the nature of Truth. A true *shastra* must therefore be full. The ancient authors have tried to achieve the fullness in a unique way: The *Shruti*, being the deposit of the self-revealed Truth, is full and hence the true means of arriving at the right notion of *dharma*. The *Smriti*, being the deposit of knowledge of the omniscient *rishi*s, becomes full by incorporating some portions of the *Shruti*. And, by accepting the sanctity of these two all other *shastra*s become full. The fullness of *shastra* can be explained in yet another way. Dealing with the universal Truth, the *Shruti* becomes full. By examining the matters of temporal life in terms of a transcendental Law, the *Smriti* becomes full. And by contextualising the eternal norms of life, all other *shastra*s become full. This means the ancient authorities have made a conscious effort toward achieving the fullness in concrete terms. The most excellent example is of the Purana, the omnibus text that describes cosmology, genealogy of Gods and illustrious kings and the events relating them, moral codes and rituals, astrology, astronomy, medicine, architecture, aesthetic principles, and all such matters as concern the four-fold aims of life (*purushartha*) and also time and divisions of time — the past, present and the future. Indeed, it is this integration of knowledge and existence that has induced an unbroken continuity of *sanatani parampara*.

4. PARISTHITI

The notion of contextualising the code of behaviour was not peculiar to the writers of the *Nibandha*. It finds its way back to the *Smriti* which had taken full cognition of the fact of change in human conditions. Most Puranas have devoted a section on the Law of the Age (*yuga dharma*) and have described in particular the characteristics of the *kali* Age, its decadent features. A number of approved usages of the ancient time are prohibited in the *kali* Age.

In the compelling situation the normal rules of conduct have been relaxed under a section of the Law called *apada-dharma*. But in no way this meant excessive and unrestricted liberty. For instance, when a brahmana is allowed to transgress the established rule of occupation at the time of crisis, he is not left at his will. The same Law restrains him:

> For the sole purpose of supporting life, let him (Brahmana) acquire property by those reproachable occupations, which are peculiar to his class, and unattended by bodily pain. — *Manu*, IV.3

> He may live by *rita* and *amrita*, or if necessary by *mrita* or *pramrita*, or even by *satyanrita*, but never let him subsist by *svavritti.* — *Manu*, IV.4

> By *rita*, must be understood lawful gleaning and gathering; by *amrita*, what is asked as alms; tillage is called *pramrita.* — *Manu*, IV.5

> Traffic and money-lending are *satyanrita*, even by them when he is deeply distressed, may he support life; but service for hire is named *svavritti*, or dog-living, and of course he must by all means avoid it. — *Manu*, IV.6

5. PARISHUDDHI

Whatever the situation, compromise with the established rules must result in *amende honorable*. The *shastra* admits change only in extreme cases, and after due deliberation and truthful consideration. For example, during the sixteenth century when temples were being destroyed in Kashi,the great Pandit Narayana Bhatta compiled a most commendable work, the *Tristhalisetu* wherein he re-interpreted the old custom of image-worship:

> Even if the self-effulgent-linga of Visheshvara (the presiding God of Kashi) is taken off somewhere and another is brought in and established by human hands, on account of the difficulty of the time, whatever is established in that place should be worshipped. And if, owing to the powers of the foreign ruler there is no *linga* at all in that place, even so the *dharma* of the place itself should be observed with rites of circumambulation, salutation, etc., and in this way the daily pilgrimage (*nitya-yatra*) shall be performed.

He quoted the *Skanda Purana*, which says:

> All the *linga*s of Kashi, be they visible, invisible, defiled (by touch pollution of the Anarya, or any person in a state of impurity), and

> broken are worthy of worship.

To emphasise on the self-purificatory system, Narayana Bhatta cited the authority of the *Sanatakumarasamhita*:

> In the early hours of the dawn Shiva takes bath in Manikarnika (a sacred spring) and performs his own worship so as to do away with the touch pollution. This he does kindly for the good of all beings in the *kali* Age.

In declaring the entire *kshetra* of Kashi as eternally sacred and all stone images worthy of worship, the sanctity of *parampara* was not only restored but actually re-vigorated. Similarly, by recognising Shiva's everyday self-purification as declared by the *Sanatakumarasamhita*, the worshipper was not only re-assured that he was worshipping the right image but also re-assured of his faith in Shiva's benevolence. The logic of the eternally sacred Kashi is in conformity with the *pauranika* description of its primeval origin; and the logic of Shiva's self-purification is drawn from the Truth of the God's omnipotency, declared both in the *Shruti* and the *Smriti*. And Narayana Bhatta's re-interpretation of the usage in the compelling situation rests on the sacred authority of the *Smriti*. Thus, when a certain Sacred Law becomes obsolete or dies out, another Sacred Law appears from the same source — duly purified by logic and sanctified by *shastra* — to live through another lifecycle. This is how the *sanatani parampara* has acquired a phoenix-like character.

Parampara: A Limiting Factor

Parampara, by definition, is changeable. Changes occur inevitably in the very process of handing down the deposit from one generation to the next. In a certain sense each generation re-organises its *parampara* in a manner which may differ slightly or significantly from the preceding generation. But changes occur within the defined and determined limits (*maryada*).

The term *maryada*, used both in the Brahmanic and the Buddhist Pali texts, denotes the rule of propriety of conduct. What has repeatedly been transmitted in the *sanatani parampara* is not to transcend the *maryada* of one's family, caste and country. And because Rama did not transcend the *maryada* of his family (*raghukula*), of his caste (kshatriya) and country (the kingdom of Ayodhya), he was called *maryada purshottama* (the best of men who did not transcend the limit). Rama preferred to live in exile than to make his father go back on his promise, because it was the *parampara* of his family to honour the words even at the cost of one's own life. Again he preferred to banish his beloved wife rather than to punish his subjects, even though he knew that his wife was in the right and his subjects were in the wrong. He did not transcend the *maryada* of a king. He banished his wife to uphold the established norms of marital life in his kingdom.

Parampara: A Three-fold Knowledge

Human life is modelled by practical experience made intelligible by Conventional Universal experience, authenticated by the criteria of Truth. In this modelling of life emerges the excellence of human organisation called *parampara*. Each generation of men contextualises the Conventional Universal experience in order to make it intelligible and operationable. Later in times, its contextualised experience becomes a conventionalised universal experience for the next generation. And backward in time are the roots of human experience — the revealed universalised transcendence — shared by every generation of men.

It follows, then, that ordinarily at no point of time can *parampara* be fully realised; it can be realised only in proportion to its intelligibility. Thus, *parampara* in its fullness remains timeless. But this timelessness of *parampara* is not to be taken as that of the pure transcendence, because it involves a co-ordination between empirical and revelatory knowledge. It may be viewed as a certain mixture of cultural reality (*vyavaharika satya*) and transcendental reality (*parmarthika satya*).

This conception of *parampara* roughly corresponds to the Brahmanic theory of knowledge which is three-fold: (1) *pratyaksha* (of particulars and generals, empirical), (2) *paroksha* (of universal, conventional), and (3) *aparoksha* (of transcendental). Of these, the first two are relative (*avidya*) and the last absolute (*vidya*). *Parampara* necessarily represents the ground of all the three. In it there is no exclusive place for pure empirical, independent of *paroksha*. Generally speaking, *parampara* is seated in *paroksha* but operates between empirical (*samvyavaharika pratyaksha*) and transcendental (*parmarthika pratyaksha*). And that indeed makes *parampara* a culturally conceivable timeless Reality.

There remains an important corollary to the main proposition which needs to be mentioned here. Both ignorance and knowledge abide in mind. *Parampara* is made of mind only. As is the mind such is the *parampara*, as is the *parampara* such is the culture. One cannot, therefore, rule out the possibility of a *parampara* of sheer 'ignorance' and the resulting 'demonic' (*asuri*) culture. Though this is theoretically conceived, it is already identified in the ancient cultures that made moral distinctions for man.

Abbreviations

GP = *Gaduda Purana*

Manu = *Manava Dharmasastra*

RV = *Rigveda*

S Bhag = *Srimada Bhagavadam*

TB = *Taittiriya Brahmana*

VP = *Vishnu Purana*

Yajn = *Yajnvalkyasmriti*

Note

This presentation is a modified version of the author's earlier paper `Thinking About Tradition: The Indian Vision' which appeared in 1986, in *Man in India* 66 (3).

2

Aspects of Parampara in Early Stages of Buddhism

M.C. Joshi

OF Sanskritic origin, the word *parampara* has been derived from the term *parampara* meaning 'one following the other' thereby denoting, broadly, transmission of beliefs, knowledge, concepts, ideas, mode of behaviour, systems, customs, etc., with or without intervals in a single or multiple form with or without adaptability. The following verse of *Srimad Bhagavad Gita* (Chapter 4, verses 2 and 3) wherein the term has been used in a specific sense gives us an idea of the revival of a *parampara* after it is lost.

> O! Arjuna this knowledge of the *yoga* revealed by Vaivasvata Manu, was received and understood by the royal sages through the *parampara*, which, however, was lost in the course of time. You being my devotee and friend, the Lord said, I would explain to you the mysteries of the same ancient *yoga*.

A further elucidation of this term is available in one of the inscriptions dating to the nineteenth regnal year (AD 149) of Pulumavi, the Satavahana ruler of Deccan which has in the expression *kulaparamparagata raja-shabdasya*, meaning that he received the title of king through *kulaparampara*, i.e., through a succession of rulers of his lineage. The term *parampara* in this case has been used in the sense of uninterrupted continuity.

Keeping in view the rise and growth of Buddhism we notice an interesting situation. Historians, invariably, believe that Gautama the Buddha of the Sakyan clan was the founder of Buddhism and headed an anti-Brahmanical movement challenging ritualism and the supremacy of the Vedas and equate him, in this respect, with Martin Luther, the foremost leader of Protestantism in Europe.

However, the textual *parampara* speaks otherwise. For instance the *Namalinganushasana* or Amarasimha, commonly known as *Amarakosha* which is a well-known Sanskrit lexicon of about the fifth century AD, mentions the term Buddha both as a common noun and as a proper name in the context of Shakyamuni or Gautama Buddha.

Thus, according to Amarasimha who is stated to be a Buddhist himself, the synonyms like a Sarvajna, Sugata, Buddha, Dharmaraja, Tathagata, Samantabhadra, Bhagavan, Marajit, Lokajit, Jina, Sadbhijna, Dasabala, Advayavadi, Vinayaka, Munindra, Shrighana, Sasta, and Muni are applicable to all the Buddhas but names like Shakyamuni, Shakyasimha, Sarvanthasiddhi, Sauddhodani, Gautama, Arkabandhu (of Solar race) and Mayadevisuta refer only to the historical Buddha.

One may argue that the tradition illustrating synonyms for Buddha in two categories, the general and the particular, being a reference in a later text may not be fully authentic, as far as early Buddhism is concerned. What, however, deserves attention in this respect is a reference in the early Pali literature (*Digha Nikaya*) to six Buddhas of human birth (*Manushi* Buddhas) in the following order viz., Vipashvi, Shikhi, Vishvabhu, Krakucchanda, Kanakamuni and Kashyapa, all of whom were precursors of the seventh Buddha Shakymuni. They have been styled as Samyakasambuddha, i.e., enlightened and preaching Buddhas as against Pratyeka Buddha, who attain enlightenment but do not expound the righteous Law to public. According to some Buddhist accounts (*Jataka Atthakatha*), Shakyamuni, while he was in the last stage of *Bodhisattva* in the heaven before his birth in the world, thought that like all the previous Buddhas he should also be born only in Madhyadesha (the sacred region covering eastern Haryana, U.P., up to parts of eastern Bihar), in Jambudvipa (India) and in either a brahmana or a kshatriya family. Thereafter, he selected for his birth, Kapilavastu as his native place, and queen Maya and king Shaddhodana of the purest Shakyan (kshatriya) race as his parents.

No doubt, it is difficult to establish the historicity and antiquity of the *Manusi* Buddhas for the absence of positive evidence. Yet we like to cite an interesting reference left by emperor Ashoka in his inscription at Nigalisagar (in Nepalese *tarai*) which records that he enlarged the *stupa* of Kanakamuni Buddha (*Konakamanasa Mune*) for the second time in his fourteenth regnal year and raised a stone column in front of the doubled structure in his twentieth year of coronation. The seven *Manushi* Buddhas including Shakyamuni are also found represented in the sculptures of Sanchi through their respective Bodhi Trees, for portrayal of Buddhas in human form was prohibited in Theravada Buddhism. Various details about the seven Buddhas are available in the *Mahopadana Sutta*, e.g., the *kalpa* (span of time) in which they take their birth, their social rank (jati), their family (*gotra*), length of life (*ayu*), the trees under which they attain enlightenment (*bodhi-vriksha*), names of their parents and chief disciples, place of birth, and number of *arhat*s in their principal assemblies. Each Buddha, according to the *parampara*, recorded in later times, achieves victory over the evil deity, Mara, delivers his first sermon at Risipatana (Isipatana or Sarnath), resides chiefly at Jetavana (Shravasti) during his lifetime and could be distinguished from others by thirty-two marks of great men on his body.

Further the Buddhist *parampara* avers that there must be a long interval of time between two human Buddhas because in the world of mortals there could be only one *Samyakasambuddha* at one time. The emergence of a new Buddha is possible only when the *shasana* of the previous Buddha has completely disappeared from the earth.

The *Buddhavamsa*, a Sri Lankan text, contains particulars of twenty-five human Buddhas, of which the last one is Gautama. The twenty-four *Tathagata*s including the celebrated Dipankara are stated to have predicted Shakyamuni's birth in the world. The Mahayanic texts like *Lalitavistara* and *Mahavastu* list, respectively, fifty-four and over a hundred human Buddhas. In the *Saddharmapundarika Sutra*, the most notable of Mahayana *shastra*s, are mentioned numerous Buddhas of whom each presides over a Buddhakshetra (region of Buddha). The Mahayana also evolved the concept of five non-human *Dhyani* Buddhas, viz., Vairocana, Akshobhya, Ratnasambhava, Amitabha and Amoghasiddhi who are often depicted on the head of Mahayanic divinities including Bodhisattvas in art. The *Dhyani* Buddhas are also supposed to have their own *devata*s and *mandala*s. A section of Mahayanic Buddhists, who were responsible for authoring the text known as *Manjushrimulakalpa*, refer to the *parampara* of Adi Buddha, i.e., Primeval Buddha, who was the first to preach the Law and to establish the Order. The subsequent Buddhas did not explore anything new but only repeated whatever was earlier expounded and practised by Adi Buddha as could be inferred from the following verses:

What has been stated by the Primeval Buddha, I retell the same

> to the travellers on the path of liberation. After saluting all the Buddhas of incomprehensible and exciting forms, I narrate the hymns intended for making offerings as unveiled by the *Samyakasambuddha*.

Both the Theravada and Mahayanic *parampara* believe that the future Buddha as the saviour of the Order is Maitreya who is presently in heaven as Bodhisattva. Details about his parents, bodhi-tree and other aspects are mentioned in *Anagatavamsa* and other texts. His concept and worship as *Bodhisattva* as well as future Buddha was very popular amongst Mahayanists in north India, Central Asia and elsewhere. His images are commonly found sculpted in Mathura and Gandhara art and also in a few paintings of Ajanta besides many Buddhist sites outside India. In early sculptures he is often shown with a jar of nectar. According to Malalasekhara, the noted Pali scholar from Sri Lanka, in some of the Buddhist manuscripts names of ten future Buddhas, e.g., Maitreya, Uttama, Rama, Prasenjit, Abhitru, Dirghayoni, Sankritya, Subha, Todeyaa and Nalagiri are found recorded. The *Saddharmapundarika Sutra* also mentions names of several devotees of Buddha, who would also attain Buddhahood in course of time.

The Buddhist *parampara* as discussed above cannot be judged historically nor is it free from mythical elements. Yet one thing is certain: that a tradition of human Buddhas seems to have been known in some form to Gautama Shakyamuni. It is not unlikely that their concept may have had some sort of linkage with the memory of some earlier sages or thinkers following *Nrivritti Marga* (i.e., path of detachment) and pursuing the ideal of *moksha* as opposed to *Pravritti Marga* associated with ritualistic Brahmanism and aiming at the attainment of heaven. The seeds of Shramanic thought are already present in *Vatarasana Sukta* of *Rigveda* and *Vratyasukta* of *Atharvaveda*.

Govinda Chandra Pande mentions several names of *Vatarasana* sages like Juti, Vatajuti, Viprajuti, Vrisanaka, Karikrita, Etasa and Rishyashringa. According to him these Shramanic sages were non-believers in god and Vedic sacrifices but upheld the law of *karman* and rebirth besides sanctity of life in any form. Such sages, it is possible, may have contributed to the rise of Buddhism which aimed at attaining highest development for a mortal outside the concept of God with an already existing *parampara*, which seems to have evolved into diverse forms and concepts including those connected with past, present and future Buddhas as a result of diversified development of Buddhism. Gautama Buddha and subsequent Buddhist *acharyas* also established certain conventions, e.g., admitting women into monkhood, use of democratic methods for decision-making and adoption of the system of raising and worshipping the *chaityas*. Subsequent Buddhist *acharyas* also introduced human image of Buddha, employment of magical formulae in rituals, and worship of numerous deities, which ultimately became incorporated into development of Buddhist *parampara*.

References

Jataka Aththakatha, ed. Fausboll *Pali Text Society*, 4, London 1877.

W.W. Rockhill, 1891, *Life of Buddha*, London.

Dighanikaya, London, *Pali Text Society*, 1890-1911.

Mahavamsa, Pali Text Society.

Buddhavamsa, Pali Text Society.

G.P. Mulalasekhara, *Dictionary of Pali, Proper Names*, Vol. I and II.

P.L. Vaidya (ed.), *Lalitavistara*, Darbhanga.

Govinda Chandra Pande, 1983, *Studies in the Origin of Buddhism*, Delhi.

Rigveda-Samhita, ed. Sripada Damodhara Satavalekar, Volumes 1-4, Svadhyaya Mandala Paradi, 1984.

Atharvaveda Samhita, ed. Sripada Damodara Satavalekar, volumes 1 to 4, Svadhyaga Mandala, Paradi 1984.

Govindra Chandra Pande, 1990, *Bauddhadharma Ke Vikas Ka Itihas*, Lucknow,.

Rahul Sankrityayana, 1954, *Buddhacharya*, Banaras.

3

Tiruppavai: A Living Parampara of Two Thousand Years

Prema Nandakumar

TRADITION has a strong hold on the Indian psyche. The Indian speaks in terms of thousands of years, not hundreds, when referring to his tradition. How did this come about? How is it that in India alone we have been able to retain traditions as ancient or more ancient than the Greek, Chinese or Japanese cultures? The terms and practices of Indians two thousand years ago are still living experiences for us. How is it that a great divide has not occurred and our ancient traditions have not become museum pieces?

Sri Aurobindo cites four instruments that have not only retained our ancient culture but have kept them vibrantly alive. He says that Indian culture had always believed in 'a firm spiritual order as well as an untrammelled freedom' and these four instruments made this a viable proposition:

> . . . in the first place on the recognition of an ever enlarging number of authorised scriptures. Of these scriptures some like the *Gita* possessed a common and widespread authority, others were peculiar to sects or schools: some like the Vedas were supposed to have an absolute, others a relative binding force. But the very largest freedom of interpretation was allowed, and this prevented any of these authoritative books from being turned into an instrument of ecclesiastical tyranny or a denial of freedom to the human mind and spirit. Another instrument of order was the power of family and communal tradition, *kuladharma*, persistent but not immutable. A third was the religious authority of the brahmanas; as priests they officiated as the custodians of

> observance, as scholars, acting in a much more important and respected role than the officiating priesthood could claim, — for to the priesthood no great consideration was given in India, — they stood as exponents of religious tradition and were a strong conservative power. Finally, and most characteristically, most powerfully, order was secured by the succession of *guru*s or spiritual teachers, *parampara*, who preserved the continuity of each spiritual system and handed it down from generation to generation but were empowered also, unlike the priest and the *pundit*, to enrich freely its significance and develop its practice.[1]

Since the Indian consciousness always strove towards a holistic view of life that integralised the secular and the sacred, every aspect of human activity came to have *parampara*s. Music, dance, sculpture, painting, religion or scientific knowledge: each has several *parampara*s. The knowledge acquired earlier was handed over to the future generation after generation with a conscious sense of the spiritual aim of our culture. Even housewifery that is generally associated with dull and mundane activities, became a sacred act - I1 + Aram, Household *dharma*. Families have their individual traditions imprinted in the tablets of the family's memory. For instance, it is not documented that women in my family must make the special lamp of rice flour once a year and light it and guard the flame for hours till it goes out. Then we bow to the lamp saying 'the Lord has gone up the Mountain, Govinda!' with the sterling belief that for these few hours Lord Venkateshvara was here as the lamp's glow. This is done on any one of the Saturdays of *Purattasi* (September-October) and the tradition was handed over to me by my mother-in-law, saying that her mother-in-law had done it as a family tradition.

One such tradition which is a family observance that has also gained wider wings of religious connotation, bridal mysticism, scholarly exegesis and artistic delineation is the *Pavai Nonbu*. The month-long *Pavai Nonbu* which concluded on 13th January this year has a *parampara* that can be traced back by two thousand years or more.

Early Tamil anthologies like *Natrinai*, *Ainkurunooru*, *Kalittokai* and *Paripadal*

---

1. *Foundations of Indian Culture*, 1953, p.149.

mention the vow of *Pavai Nonbu* as *Thai Neeradal* (bathing in the month of *Thai*). *Paripadal* describes it as a popular ceremony performed by young girls. They rise at dawn, go to the river Vaigai and take a purificatory bath in its cool waters during the month of *Thai* (January-February) and pray for various marital blessings and eat a specially cooked meal:

> 'O water of Vaigai! You are crystalline,
> Hence I bathe in you', say some girls;
> 'May my beloved embrace me
> With arms entwined', pray a few;
> 'My loving consort shouldn't leave me
> Like the bee that rejects the used-up flower.
> That joy of union be mine', pray some;
> 'Let not old age mar our youth's bliss.
> May we have prosperity and relatives,
> Pray some other maidens.[2]

No doubt the framework of the ceremony described in the ancient *Paripadal* was used by Andal to describe her soul's yearnings in the *Tiruppavai* (*c.* eighth century AD) and added to similar rites mentioned in the stories current about Krishna's life which were later documented as the *Bhagavata Purana*. The *Bhagavata* says:

> At the beginning of the *Hemanta* (winter season) the maidens of Vraja observed the vows connected with the worship of Katyayani subsisting only on sacrificial food. 'O King! Bathing in the river at sunrise, they installed a sand image of the Devi on the bank of the Kalindi and worshipped Her with sandal paste, garlands of sweet smelling flowers, incense, light, sprouts of leaves, fruits, cereals, and food offerings of various kinds.' 'O Devi Katyayani! Thou mighty cosmic power and mistress of all! Deign to make Nanda's son my husband. My salutations to Thee!' Repeating this Mantra, these maidens of Vraja worshipped the Devi.[3]

2. Translated by Prema Nandakumar.
3. Translated by Swami Tapasyanananda, *Srimad Bhagavata*: *The Holy Book of God*, Vol. III., p. 132.

The Krishna legends also have a rite similar to the *Pavai* Nonbu and *Katyayani vrata*. Once there was a drought in the Yadava country because the elderly Yadavas hid their maidens in cellars as they thought that Krishna's amorous nature might affect them. Either due to the good time the *gopi*s had had with Krishna, or due to Varuna frowning at this uncalled for insinuation, rains failed and there was severe drought. The cowherds got together and decided that the girls were to observe an ancient rite for the coming of rains. They requested Krishna to conduct the rite as he only knew its methodology. He refused but agreed after repeated urgings. Krishna took the cowherdesses to the banks of Yamuna and after a while asked them to go back home while he himself went to the palace of Nappinnai. The girls who could not bear the separation went as a group to Nappinnai's palace and received the Lord's grace and brought the rite to fruition.[4]

As the foster-daughter of Perialwar, Andal was brought up in an atmosphere of Krishna's legends. Historically, she is assigned to the eighth century. M. Raghava Iyengar has worked upon a statement in the thirteenth verse of *Tiruppavai* — 'the planet Venus has risen, the planet Jupiter has set' — pertaining to a full moon day early in the morning and arrived at AD 716 as the year of her birth.[5] Since her foster-father Perialwar lived in the days of Parantaka Nedunchadayan (AD 750-90), eighth century is a plausible date.

Perialwar was a hymnologist and perhaps it was quite natural for Andal to write poetry in that domestic atmosphere. The 143 verses in her *Nachiar Tirumoli* and the 30 verses in the *Tiruppavai* are soulful devotionals. Her own life was one of total dedication to the Divine. After telling her father that she would not care to marry an ordinary mortal she led a life of devotional ecstasy and gained the ineffable vision of the Lord at Shrirangam. After such a union, time and space were annihilated and the devotee became one with the deity.

Thus, 173 verses of Andal is all that we have. All of them are hymns of bridal mysticism. Seen in the background of the earlier literature of the Tamils, Andal's work affords a fine example of how a great tradition is made to enrich the nation in newer and higher ways of thought and emotional identity. The *Tiruppavai* is an instance of how the *Thai Neeradal* of ancient Tamils became the

4. See K. Srinivasa Iyengar, 1991, *Tiruppavai Vyakhyanam*, pp. 19-20.

5. *Alwarkal Kalanilai*, p. 76.

Margazhi Nonbu of later times. As with the other Sangham conventions, the *Thai Neeradal* ceased to be a prayer for good husbands and was transformed into a rite to invoke the Grace of Krishna, unite with Him and pledge one's life to eternal servitude to Him. When it was made a part of the *Nalayira Divya Prabhandam* by Acharya Nathamuni, the poem gained scriptural authority for the Vaishnavites. It became an instrument used for recitation, meditation, ritualistic observance and scholarly exegesis.

This *parampara* of *Tiruppavai* has become inextricably entwined with the life of the Shrivaishnava way of life. That is the reason why though she signs herself as 'Kothai' in her poems, she is better known as Andal or 'one who rules us'. The *Tiruppavai* is recited and expounded during the *Margashirsha* month and the rituals are followed with some inevitable local variations. During the thirty days of *Margashirsha*, men and women in orthodox Shrivaishnavite homes bathe before dawn, cook rice with *dal* as an offering to the Lord, and recite the *Tiruppavai* and also other verses from the *Prabhandham*. Lectures are arranged in the mornings and evenings and the *Tiruppavai* verses are expounded one on each day till the verse garland concludes on the day prior to *Makara Sankranti*. On this day, known as *bhogi* day, the marriage of Andal and Lord Ranganatha is celebrated with enthusiasm in temples as well as in specially erected *pandal*s. Regional enthusiasm gives variety too. I have myself participated in the *Margashirsha vrata* festivals arranged by Shri Lakshmana Yateendra of Mumukshu Peetham in Andhra Pradesh. On the bhogi day, the Yateendra would order for large pots filled with curds and it was exhilarating for the assembled audience to take part in the churning, drawing the ropes of large wooden churners. The smell of fresh butter would permeate the place and everybody would be in a state of joy, as if they had gone back to the cowherd settlement of Gokula in Krishna's time. It may also be mentioned that on the 27th day we celebrate with rice cooked with milk and jaggery and plentiful of *ghee* as an offering, to indicate how one was drawing close to the conclusion of the *vrata*:

Vanquisher of foes, Govinda! O Sublime One!
Let these be our rewards
For singing and serving you.
Presents praised by the world;
Jewels for the wrists and shoulders

> Ear-rings and ear-flowers; anklets too.
> We would then sit together, comfortably cool,
> And enjoy rice cooked with milk
> Overflowing with *ghee* that would
> Drip down our elbows.[6]

As a child of Tamil heritage who also imbibed the *Bhagavata* traditions from the North, Andal wrote the *Tiruppavai* as a guidance-hymn for those who wished to follow the path of devotion. A seasonal rite had been transformed by her into a religious vow leading the aspirant to enter the shoreless seas of mystic at-one-ment with the Divine. The poem no doubt contains prayers for rains, cattle and prosperity, but as Andal makes it clear, the final aim is to gain the Grace (*parai*) of the Lord.

It was the good fortune of the Vaishnava community that the *Nalayira Divya Prabhandham* which was revered as a scripture had a great *parampara* of teachers who ceaselessly commented upon the verses generation after generation. Unlike the Sanskrit Vedas which do not have a standard interpretation and the Thevaram hymns by Shaivite Nayanmars (who were close contemporaries of the Alwars), every word of the *Nalayira Divya Prabhandham* hymns has been expounded carefully by a succession of *acharya*s ever since Ramanujacharya presented the *Ubhaya Vedanta* concept. The commentary tradition for *Tiruppavai* begins with Peria Achan Pillai (twelfth century), and we may safely say that his *Moovayirappadi* consolidated the place of *Tiruppavai* in the religious observances of the Vaishnavites and saw to it that the thirty verses in the poem are not stray outpourings but a regular dramatic argument. But for his opening bars, the *Tiruppavai* may have remained an obscure poem for us. We may still have blindly followed the observance but would have been lost in myopic faith and ritualism.

Tiruppavai is about a group of young maidens going from house to house bidding their friends rise and join them for an early morning bath. Andal imagines that she is a cowherdess in the settlement of Gokula. This ideational change reflects in other transformations. The temple of Vatapatrasayi in Srivillipputtur becomes the palace of Nandagopa. Krishna's exploits in many of his incarnations are recaptured with affection and admiration. A feeling of abundance, happiness

---

6. Translated by R. Bangaruswami.

and aspiration marks Andal's tone and rich diction.

The first verse of *Tiruppavai* itself refers to the rite as the *Margazhi-Neeradal*, not *Thai-Neeradal* as in the *Sangham* poems. This is the auspicious dawn of *Margashirsha* (December-January), auspicious because the Lord has said in the *Gita* that this is the best month of the year. Also, M. Raghava Iyengar says that the discrepancy in the naming of the month is because of a change from the lunar to the solar calender in Tamil Nadu. The rite is to conclude on a Full Moon day and this is in tune with the observation of *Tiruvatirai* Festival in Kerala and *Arudhra Darshan* by Shaivites in Tamil Nadu. Thus the *Margazhi Nonbu* is but a transformation of the ancient Tamil *Thai Neeradal*.

The second verse gives the code of discipline for those who take up the rite. There is no troublesome ritualism. The stress is on personal purity, both external and internal:

> Oh, people of the world! Lend your ears
> To the code of our ritual,
> Singing the glories of our gently-sleeping Lord
> Floating on the milky sea,
> We will refrain from taking milk or *ghee*,
> Apply no collyrium to our eye or wear flowers.
> No wrongful things will we do or say.
> But take our morning bath and do acts of charity
> As the best way to life and prosperity.[7]

First of the injunctions is a constant remembrance of the Lord: 'singing the glories of the gently-speaking Lord'. This is followed by avoiding food that creates sloth or grossness. Time should not be wasted in personal decorations. Most important of all, one must avoid evil speech and action. By avoiding evil thoughts and filling oneself with the vision of Vasudeva, a rare compassion would fill our heart towards all creation. Acts of charity come naturally to such a person. Those who wish to live in the world (*vaiyattu vazveerkaal*) must follow this code. Those who do not do so are but animated dolls. The promises held out by the observance of the rite are listed in the third verse: there will be properly

7. Translated by R. Bangaruswami

planned rains (not too little, not too much), rich paddy yield, big, generous cows that would fill the pots and endow ample wealth.

The fourth verse is a prayer to Varuna for copious rains and the fifth is an assurance that a pure life accompanied by total surrender to the Divine would see to it that the errors of the past (committed knowingly or in ignorance) would be destroyed for ever. Surrender to the Divine means a constant remembrance: sing of the Lord, worship him with pure flowers, meditate upon the All-Beautiful Delight of Existence!

In the following ten verses, ten girls are awakened with a mix of pleadings and feigned anger. In the sixteenth verse, all the girls come to Nandagopa's palace and request the guards to open the gates. In the course of the six verses that follow, Nandagopa, Yashoda, Krishna, Balarama and Nappinnai are awakened. The twenty-third verse reveals the Lord awake 'like the lion that has slept through the rainy season, and is now coming out of the cave, fully conscious with fiery eyes'. Four more verses prayerfully seek the *purusharthas*. The twenty-eighth hymn reminds one of Arjuna's reaction to the Lord's *vishvarupa*, the recognition of the Divine in one who was till then but a companion in life:

> We will follow the cows to the wood
> And dine there. Born though in this clan
> That boasts of no enlightenment,
> We have the fortune to have you amongst us.
> Govinda, untouched by the least blemish!
> Our relations do not terminate here
> Ignorant folks we, in our love
> We called you by familiar names.
> No offence please! Grant us boons.[8]

The verse that follows assures Krishna that despite knowing his true form, there will be no change in the attitude of the devotees for they have made a complete surrender to him. Though they had been saying that the rite was undertaken to get the *parai-drum* (a symbol betokening the *purusharthas*), it is the *parai* of whole-hearted service to the Lord that has been their goal. This

8. Translated by R. Bangaruswami

desire to be the Lord's servitor is the very essence of Shrivaishnavism:

> He (the aspirant) should pray that God Himself should eliminate the obstacles that will crop up in the attainment of the highest end and in the understanding of the true nature of self and of the effective means of realising the objective, namely the Supreme Self. The principal purpose of this ritual, as also of life, is to be in the ever-enchanting presence of the Lord. The *gopika*s have made a clear enunciation of what their intentions are in undertaking the rite and how they have fulfilled them, so as to enable us to find a way of salvation for ourselves.[9]

The final verse is a *phala shruti*. Those who recite this verse-garland in the right order in the same manner of emotional identification inspired by Andal will gain the Lord's grace. Because of the continued observance of the *Margashirsha vrata* (*Margali Nonbu*, *Sri vrata*) by a large number of devotees even today, the *Tiruppavai* remains a living force. It may be pointed out that even though several centuries have passed by and there have been several commentaries in many languages, the adherence to the *parampara* of *manipravala* exegesis begun by Peria Achan Pillai has not been questioned at all. Further significances may have been added, but the thread of argument that he found in the thirty verses has had no challengers.

Going back to the first exegesis, we find that the reason is not far to seek. The magnificent intellect of Peria Achan Pillai, backed by enormous scholarship in Sanskrit works and an intense devotion for the *Alwar*s, has given us something more than a classic in *Moovayirappadi*. The work has scriptural power and is the firm, rock-like basis for all future commentaries as the great guide of the *Tiruppavai parampara*.

The first thing to note about Peria Achan Pillai's commentary is his unswerving devotion to Andal and the prime place he gives her in the *Alwar-Acharya*s pantheon. Though she is neither the first nor the oldest of the *Alwar*s, her devotion is considered to belong to the highest plane. Strangely enough, it is Andal's gender that gives her this prime position proving that women may be at a disadvantage in politics, trade, social life and art, but in the realm of *Bhakti*

9. S. Applacharyulu, 1980, *Tiruppavai*, p. 504.

Yoga, they reign supreme:

> The difference between sages who have attained realisation and people engaged in secular pursuits (in the matter of at-one-ment with the Supreme) is that between a mountain and an atom. The same difference may be said to exist between the *Alwar*s and the sages. Such a vast difference is found between Perialwar and the rest of the *Alwars*. So too between Andal and Perialwar.[10]

According to Peria Achan Pillai this was because Andal took an active part in waking up the Lord and informing him of the need of the devotees and as good as coerced him into granting grace to the helpless children of mortality. He was no doubt following the lead of Ramanujacharya who had said that Andal carried all the spiritual attainment of the rest of the *Alwar*s as her *stri-dhan* and had gifted the Lord with a rare clarity of perception by giving him an accurate idea of His own creation.

As with the *acharya*s of Shrivaishnavism in those distant days, Peria Achan Pillai proceeded to link Andal and *Tiruppavai* with the religious-spiritual literature belonging to the Vedic *parampara*. The *Ramayana* is a major inspiration for 'placing' Andal and the *Tiruppavai*. Though Tamil literature was equally ancient, it was more secular in nature and there is very little of *bhakti* literature pertaining to Vishnu and his incarnations in the *Sangham* works. Hence, it is Sanskrit works that get cited often, as Ramanujacharya had also written in Sanskrit. But the wonderful Tamil hymns of the *Alwar*s are quoted profusely. Only phrases are given, probably because the listeners of Peria Achan Pillai could immediately remember the rest of the verse, as they were all familiar with the hymns in the *Nalayira Divya Prabhandham*, considered as the Tamil Veda (*Tamizh Marai*) and the *Ramayana* of Valmiki. It was considered a holy act to memorise these two works completely. Intertwining of Sanskrit and Tamil as the *Manipravala* gives *Moovayirappadi* a sprightly strength, which is unique.

Yet another important lead given by Peria Achan Pillai is to quote his own teachers and contemporaries, of their experiences. The effect is immediate, dramatic. For example, while explaining the fifteenth verse, he says that it is no good to forget the Vaishnava ambience and have connections with people who

---

10. Translated by Prema Nandakumar.

go after other gods. 'Remember Alwan' is his injunction. The commentators who came after him have explained this statement with what had actually happened to Alwan. When Ramanuja had gone away to Tirunarayanapuram due to persecution from King Krimikatha, his disciple Alwan happened to go to the Shrirangam temple. He was stopped from entering by a few, but others intervened and said he may be allowed in. On Alwan's query he was told that Ramanuja's friends and disciples had been barred from the temple. Alwan turned back saying 'I do not want the Lord (Perumal); I wish only closeness to my teacher, Ramanuja'.

The *Tiruppavai Kalakshepa parampara* has followed this habit with great success and hence, the past has been conserved very well and rich additions of *bhagavad anubhava* have also been made. Languages may be different in the exposition of *Tiruppavai* these days, but the speaker prefers to follow strictly the basic ideas and even phrases, embellishing the same with his own imagination and experience.

One example should suffice. Here is the fifth verse of the *Tiruppavai*:

> Child of North Mathura Maya incarnate,
> Sporting in the holy waters of Yamuna!
> Lustrous lamp of the cowherd clan!
> Purifier of your mother's womb! Damodara!
> If we but approach you with purity,
> Worship you with flowers pure,
> Sing your praises with deep emotion,
> And meditate upon you in our minds,
> Our past errors and those that creep in future
> will burn like cotton in the fire.[11]

Peria Achan Pillai imagines a background for this verse where a *gopika* speaks to her friends (they have just prayed to Varuna for copious rains) that though one may have faith in the rite, is it possible to complete the same? Even great sages have failed to achieve their goal:

> One of the girls questioned: We have begun the rite with great hopes.

11. Translated by R. Bangaruswami.

> Where is the certainty that this *vrata* would be completed? Will not the *karma*s accumulated from times immemorial prove to be a hurdle? Is it not said, *sreyamsi bahu vignani*? One of them who had knowledge of the *shastra*s (*vedanta jnana*) replied: 'It is not imperative to remove our sins first and then begin the *vrata*. Experience of the Divine (*bhagavad anubhava*) will automatically chase away sins even as bile flees from a man when he drinks milk. Hence one need not avoid the rite feeling unworthy to undertake the same.'[12]

The imagined situation must be an authentic one for the hold of *parampara* is very deep in the Indian psyche. Though Ramanujacharya said that no one can comment upon Andal's *Tiruppavai* as it has innumerable inlaid coils of meaning, he was himself propagating the poem and was known as *Tiruppavai Jeeyar*. He must have received the dramatic background that binds the thirty verses together from the *acharya*s who had been on the scene earlier (*poorvai acharya*s) spreading Shrivaishnavism and thus the lineage could be traced back to Andal herself. Those who came after him (like Nampillai) became the links. Nampillai was the teacher of Peria Achan Pillai. The commentary proceeds with a word-for-word explanation drawing generously from earlier literature, myths, legends. 'Mayan', the first word of the verse, takes the commentator to the *paratva* and *saulabhya* of the Lord. He is *Mayan* because he is the Supreme and is yet accessible. He is so accessible as to give himself completely to the denizens of the cowherd settlement. In the course of commenting upon this verse, Peria Achan Pillai quotes from the *Alwar*s, the Vedas, the *Vishnu Purana*, and the *Ramayana*.

It may be pointed out here that despite the thick layers of Sanskrit quotations, Peria Achan Pillai's commentary is easy to read and understand. It was good he recorded the *Moovayirappadi* commentary. The *Arayirappadi* extends and explicates what Peria Achan Pillai has said in a likeable style. Alakiya Perumal Nayanar gives just a welcome push to the argument to dramatise the statements of his predecessors. Whereas Peria Achan Pillai refers to the accessibility of *Krishnavatara*, Nayanar adds: 'he incarnated as Krishna so that anyone could bind him and beat him'. In the earlier commentary there was just a reference to the phrase, sreyamsi bahu vijnai. Nayanar gives the exact reference from the Ramayana.

---

12 Translated by Prema Nandakumar.

> Sreyamsi bahu vijnani, it is said that even the noblest have many hurdles on their path. Dasharatha, the destroyer of Sambhara, prepares for the crowning of the Lord. Vasishta who made the Rajarishi into a Brahmarishi indicates the auspicious time. The Lord who is all-auspicious and is hailed as 'Ramo vigrahavan Dharmah' is to be crowned. The Lord with his consort went to worship, *'saha pathnya visalakshya narayanamupagamth'*. Praying for the crowning, the entire land looks forward to the event, 'we desire', *icchamaha*. But even that was stopped. We have sins accumulated from times immemorial. So can we hope to achieve our goal?

Then Nayanar explains that the Lord himself will remove the hurdles even if it means trouble for himself. He had not been crowned because he wished to crown Sugriva and Vibhishana. He guarded his devotee Arjuna by taking to arms, telling lies and transforming day into night.

Both *Eerayirappadi and Nalayirappadi* were set down by Jananyachar. Though brief, his commentaries draw the reader-listener deeper into the subject. *Mayan* the Supreme is illimitable like 'Kaveri that cannot be bound', says Jananyachar, revealing his pride in the river on whose banks he lived. As for the worry of the *gopika* that there may be hurdles, Jananyachar simply says: 'There may be hurdles to what the Lord plans; but no hurdles come in the way of the plans formed by the Lord's devotees.' Other commentators who sought to unveil significances in the pattern set by *Moovayirappadi* include Suddha Satvam Doddacharya, the Jeeyar of Vanamamalai Mutt.

There are also other commentaries written about 200 years ago as the ones by Peria Parakalaswami and Sri Ranganathaswami. There are alternate readings and continued attempts to relate Andal and her work with the Vedas. For instance, Peria Parakalaswami assures us that the name *Goda* shows that what we find in Tiruppavai are no simple verses of prayer but mantric chants of illimitable potency. *Gaam sukthim dattavati yaa saa Goda: Goda* is the one who grants us a clear perception of *tattva, hita* and *purushartha.*

After beginning thus, Peria Parakalaswami moves forward to relate Andal with the concept of Mother Lakshmi as teacher. She is also Bhu Devi, Neela Devi. She was Sita in *treta yuga*, Rukmini in *dvapara yuga* and was now acting out in *Tiruppavai* the days of Krishna in Gokula through songs and worship. Her repetition of 'yel-or-empavai' is explained as an advice-*cum*-command: Do understand this verse's sound-patterns if you wish to possess the Lord. This underlining of the importance of sounds (*chandas*) itself is an indication of the *mantric* power encapsulated in *Tiruppavai*.

Just as the *mantra* sinks in the *yogin*'s ear and inspires incandescent visions, the commentators grow ecstatic, listening to the verses which act as a cinematograph. By the time of Parakalaswami, the *Alankara Shastra* gives a hand too and a *gopika* is said to be a *prowda nayaki* (verse ten):

> In fact, so keen are her ways that Krishna calls out for help! The other girls sense this according to Parakalaswami: 'Look at her gaining him by a single leap of the *vrata* when we have been doing nothing but bathing and performing *vratas*! And now she will not care to say a word even! Was Kumbhakarna defeated by her and did he surrender his sleep to her? If it were so, the sleep would be for only six months in a year (which was Kumbhakarna's time-table). But her sleep knows no end!'

While explaining the 28th verse, Ranganathaswami scours the entire Vedic, Upanishadic and Itihasic literature to indicate the nature of the Supreme (*satyam-jnanam-anantam-brahma; anando brahma*; *adiyavarnam tamasah parasthat; maharajanam vasah*) that yet cares to incarnate as a humble cowherd in this settlement, and gets lost in wonderment. The Lord's friendliness is so sweet that he is quite pleased with the cowherd ways of talking, eating and grazing cattle. Sri Ranganathaswami finds in this single verse all the limbs of *prapatti* including a tremendous faith, *mahavishvasa*.

Which is, in a way, true of each of the verses of *Tiruppavai*. Like Indra's necklace of pearls, each pearl reflecting all the rest, in *Tiruppavai*, each verse relates to all the other twenty-nine *pasurams*. For as Sri Ranga Ramanujaswami indicates in the prefatory note to his Sanskrit translation of the poem, this is a work written by the Divine Mother Compassion herself (*kshamasambhuta*) who had incarnated in the image of Andal in the household of Perialwar. The commentatorial *parampara* which perhaps began in Andal's own time and was set to the written tablet by Peria Achan Pillai continues still.

4

Parampara in Indian Music

Prem Lata Sharma

Parampara is translated as tradition, but both are not identical in connotation. Whereas 'tradition' implies a static set of knowledge, skill, beliefs, *parampara* is a dynamic flow that has room for change, innovation and individual preference.

While nobody claims novelty or originality in *parampara* (the Pauranika *parampara* is a case in point here), it is equally true that the talented individual does add, subtract or innovate and thus the *parampara* gets constantly enriched.

Parampara is an abstraction just like 'society'. The concrete entity is the individual. The abstraction naturally subsists in the group of individuals concerned. A majority of the individuals follow the beaten track but a minority of talented ones make a mark by enriching the existing corpus of knowledge or skill. It is difficult to analyse what the individual has inherited and what he has added but this process of amalgamation is perennial.

In Indian music, knowledge and skill is transmitted orally. In the initial stages of training, the student is required to imitate or reproduce whatever the teacher sings or plays, but soon enough one is guided towards doing improvisation on one's own. Needless to say, this improvisation is based on *parampara*. It is impossible to pinpoint the beginning of a *parampara* and hence, a given *parampara* is a blending of what is termed *anadi* (beginningless) and what is ascribed to a specific individual. One of the qualities of a musician is said to be his belonging to a good *sampradaya*,[1] which could be roughly equated with *parampara*.

Sampradaya has been defined as

1. *SR* III. 18ab

> he who knows properly, what he says in essence is said to constitute *sampradaya.*

Another definition is

> whatever has been said here and there is set into a system having a specific sequence, and is known as *sampradaya*, just like gold ornaments that are handed down from generation to generation (in a family).[2]

The above two definitions indicate the following characteristics of *sampradaya*:

(i) There is somebody who knows something properly and speaks out the essence of this knowledge. His knowledge itself should be understood to be composed of what he has inherited and what he has supplemented. His own understanding and manner of transmission is important.

(ii) A system is formulated from scattered pieces of knowledge or skill and this system has a specific sequential formulation.

(iii) The sense of handing over from generation to generation is also there.

Thus, a system of knowledge or skill is a combination of anonymous flow and specific individual contribution. The analogy of a river and its tributaries that become part of the river and cannot be separated from it, can give some idea of the flow of *parampara*.

The case of Pt. Omkarnath Thakur could be taken as an illustration here. He was a disciple of Pt. Vishnu Digambar Paluskar but stood out distinctly among his fellow-students of the same *guru*. Once a proposal was presented before him that his *jugalbandi* with two of his *guru-bhai*s should be arranged. The reply that he gave is very significant:

> 'Your proposal is very good, very laudable, it would be great if it could be feasible. They are great musicians and it would be an honour to sing with them. It would be a great tribute to Guruji, but it is not possible. . . .' 'Yes, we are all disciples of the same great Guru, yet with the passage of time we have drifted far

---

2. Anonymous citation in the *Sudhakara* commentary of Simhabhupala on *SR* VII.90.

> apart. They are purists and have ably kept the tradition of Guruji alive. I went along my own way. I studied many texts, learned music from many sources, even from folk music. I studied Bharata's *Natyashastra* and learnt the *kaku prayoga* (use of the inflection of voice). These studies added *abhinaya* (acting) to my music. I have tried to visualise the *raga-ragini*s. I have searched in the realm of music for *nayaka-nayika*s. I am an experimentalist. . . .[3]

His devotion to his guru was unshakeable but he enriched his style with emotive input.

> Another assessment of his deviation or innovation would be interesting, The first striking feature which brought him into relief when compared to his *guru-bhai*s (other disciples of his own *guru*), such as Vinayak Rao Patwardhan or Narayan Rao Vyasa, was Omkarnathji's remarkable evocative use of voice. In the case of the two stalwarts mentioned (and in fact many others in the larger Gwalior musical approach itself), a certain sameness of tone pervaded, irrespective of scale-ranges traversed, musical genre selected or *raga* elaborated. To maintain an even and minimally distorted vowel 'a' was an ideal tenaciously pursued, reasons being historico-cultural, aesthetic as well as those attributable to physical and external conditions related to performance. As a consequence, there was only a negligible trace of modulation of voice, an effect well-described in Indian musicology as *svara-kaku*. On the other hand, Omkarnathji sensed the significance of the diversion of timbre as indispensable to music-making. He was interested in, as also the necessity of exploring and exploiting the aspect of quality in voice. From his generation, it would be difficult to point to another vocalist who used so much variety, purposefulness and skill in employing tonal colour. A special dramatic touch pervasive in his music is discernible as the technique of presenting music in which musical content is shaped through phrasing inherent in an act of speech. In his music as

3. Extract from Dr. Bhanu Shankar Mehta's article entitled, "His Gayaki - Deviations and Innovations", in *Shruti*, no.157, October'97, p.27.

> well as in his communicative techniques, Omkarnathji comes out as a major deviationist.[4]

The amalgamation of anonymity and specific contribution in *parampara* is again visible here. Pt. Vishnu Digambar Paluskar was trained by Pt. Balakrishna Bua Ichalakaranjikar who, in turn, was trained at Gwalior. The origin of the Gwalior *gharana* or *parampara* is traceable to the first half of the nineteenth century but naturally it could not have originated in a vacuum and its background is somewhat shrouded in anonymity. Vishnu Digambarji made a mark by his crusade against the social stigma attached to those involved with music-making. Omkarnathji carried forward this crusade in his own way. His study of *Natya-shastra* and his own understanding of the relationship between speech and music enabled him to develop a unique style. His study of Sanskrit, Hindi, Gujarati and Marathi literatures intensified his understanding of the evocative power of music. This understanding got a full scope of actual application when he composed two 'operas' based on the Hindi poet, Jayashankar Prasad's *Kamayani* (epic) and *Kamana* (prose play) in 1950 and 1952 respectively. He took special care that the music composed by him matched the various mental states depicted in the above two pieces of literature. Not only that, he also depicted through his music the spatial relationship between the characters in different situations.

His music was a glowing illustration of the fact that innovation and deviation was possible and effective in the framework of *parampara*. He did not have to change the patterns of *raga*s and *tala*s, but his creativity could find full scope within that framework.

In Conclusion, the case of Pt. Omkarnath Thakur illustrates that the phenomena of deviation and innovation is a natural part of any *parampara*. For some time the contribution of specific individuals can be discerned in a *parampara* but eventually this contribution is assimilated in the *parampara* concerned and becomes part of it. It is impossible to calculate how much remains for posterity and how much is lost out of such deviations and innovations. Just as the origins of a *parampara* lie in anonymity, similarly individual contributions eventually merge into anonymity.

---

4. Excerpts from Prof. Ashok Ranade's article entitled, 'His Music: An Assessment', in *Shruti*, no. 157. October '97, pp. 45-48.

SR = *Sangita Ratnakara* of Sarangadeva (early thirteenth century AD)

5

The Parampara Predicament

Raghava R. Menon

LIKE so many words that we have inherited unexamined from our past, the *parampara* too is used in a loose profane sense when we find it sufficient to call it tradition, as something that has been repeated many times across a few generations. In actual fact, if we look at it closely there is no English word that can be substituted for the word *parampara* as an adequate and sufficient description.

A family history of epilepsy or diabetes or any other affliction recurring in some fashion across a few generations would not be a *parampara* although loosely we do call it that. It would not even be properly a tradition although marrying young in some families could be construed as one.

The word tradition therefore would not do. The reason is that the concept of *parampara* does not exist in the culture of the West. This word comes out of a typically Indian understanding of man and his true place on earth. The problem is that in the Indian context you cannot believe in the *parampara*. For all beliefs in the Indian inheritence is false unless they become experience. And once a belief has become an experience it is no longer a belief but a truth. Beliefs however passionately held have no place in a *parampara*.

The word *parampara* is based on an Indian experience. Obviously this experience is built on what the Indian inheritance defines as life, and what it considers as man's place in it. *Parampara* too, like the words *tyaga* and *samnyasa*, belongs to that family of words which mechanical and careless usage has degraded to a base level of grasp and awareness; as a result, these words are today little understood and half-believed and reduced to nothing more than half-truths.

It is in the same class of words like *svara*. Like tradition which we use to describe the *parampara*, we use the word `note' for the word *svara*. But every one who has the slightest understanding of *svara*, knows that it is not a note. The technique outside the world of experience to get at the bottom of the meanings of commonly used words is to go to the root of the Sanskrit word from which it is derived and find how the word is built. The root section of the word *para*, has the section *pa* for which there are about ten meanings. It also says the root *pa* stands for protection, to save, to defend, to keep safe. The part *sva* of the word *svara* means Self and the part *ra* means to shine forth, radiance, to bestow. The word *svara* then becomes the quality of bestowing or shining of the Self. The same technique would show that the *pa* section of the word *para* would be the bestowing of protection or the protection of the radiance. After all the Egyptian Sun God is also called *ra*, so it is not difficult to believe that the word *ra* as radiance is likely.

One of the reasons why *svara sadhana* is possible in music is because of the fact that the *svara sadhana* does not make you a musician as much as it makes you cultivate a Self which you ordinarily do not possess. And it is this self which shines out of your art that makes *raga vidya* almost divine. In this context, the protection of the illumination which is the *para* of *parampara* becomes credible as experienced.

Sanskrit grammarians detest this kind of word making out of the roots of ancient concepts. It is derisively called *Meccanoing* a word. Perhaps there is a point in sticking to the common usage of words which collect a lot of grime and glaze through careless use over the centuries.

This is particularly true for someone who has had no experience of the action of the *parampara* in his own life; for such a person, the unregenerate word tradition should be enough to get by. But those who have had a personal experience of the curious nature of this inheritence as a technique of transmission, know the difference. They know that the *parampara* has no direct use of knowledge as information. The *parampara* is concerned with the transformation of man. This is among the reasons why when you ask a musician who is a product of a *parampara* to explain a *raga* to you he would always say 'I can sing and show it to you'. It is the proof of the pudding in such cases. This too is one of the reasons why in ancient India brahmanas were kept out of life by feeding them on sight, by being made into scholars and priests and the learners of the original texts so that they become the libraries of the social order. This is why brahmanas traditionally are more prone to quote from Sanskrit scriptures and general reading whenever placed in need to express an idea for they have none of their own, being prevented from even touching others for fear of being polluted. Quotations make all of life's many perplexities seem already dealt with, in full, and life seems self-evident. The need to live it and test things out for oneself had been delegated to the rest of society.

The *parampara* therefore is directed to the individual alone, to one mechanism to find a new and throbbing awareness of vast truths without having to learn it. The word of mouth is the consequence of this understanding. Such a tradition can only be oral; the touch and the feel of a boundless presence is the *guru*, who is a way rather than the source. He tells you how and never what.

6

Parampara and Poetry: Ambiguity of the Charmed Word

Sitakant Mahapatra

POETIC creativity is destined to have an ambivalent relationship with language and hence, with *parampara* or tradition, whichever way it is defined. This destiny, in fact, is unique to all literary creativity. In other forms of creativity, such as the visual arts or the performing arts, the basic tools of colour or sound are available to the creator as nascent elements ready to be shaped, fashioned and designed in any unique way in the crucible of his imagination. They have not acquired a solid historical presence and communitarian meaning. Colour, after all, is historically indeterminate, socially neutral. So too is sound. That gives operational freedom to the creator's imagination to play with them around the creative fire. In their various combinations, juxtapositions and marriages they generate myriad unique forms and shapes. The act of creativity is directed only to the discovery of a shape, a form out of the multiple possible permutations and combinations of colours and sounds. Even though not determined or shaped by history and society they are autonomous in their own ways. They may refuse particular mixings and placements in given contexts. But finding how they, in their placements, can create the form, and the structure that he/she is envisaging is after all the task of the visual artist or the musician. One is lucky only to the extent of having his building-blocks of creativity given to him/her as an undetermined and original possession.

Not so the writer and the poet. For a poet each word in the poem has to be original and unique. But each word that he can use comes loaded with a cultural baggage, impregnated by history, and a whole multitude of murmuring nuances and the light of suggestion or *dhvanyaloka.* At the moment of use in the poem, however, the poet wants each word to be totally unique, as though it has just been born, as though he is the first to give it a name, a habitation, a colour, a context, a signifance. But he is simultaneously aware of the word's whisperings, its other connections, linkages, habitats, and significations. Octavio Paz goes to the extent of saying that 'poetic creation begins as a violence to the language'. What he implies is that given the kind of situation just described, the uprooting of the word from history and social commonality and its installation in the charmed world of uniqueness that the poet wants to create becomes inevitable. The poet is also destined to return the word to its fold of commonality for he is not creating a poem purely as an act of self-possession or as a mantra to be recited for an absent god. The poem is created, after all, for readers who have to read, re-create and relive the poem's experiential context as much as its verbal portfolio. The poem with all its words has to be parked in a land of familiar usages and commonalities, a world of inevitable dilutions due to variegated meaning and nuances imposed by and consistent with multiple readers and their individual perceptions of reality.

Human civilisation is a record of the relationship between words and thought. And no one knows the problem of this relationship more intensely, no one has felt it in his blood more deeply, than a sensitive poet. History throws up ideas, thoughts and perceptions concerning life and reality. These perceptions are conceptualised into dogmas, ideologies and theories. At the social level words acquire the smell of these dogmas and ideologies like butter in the refrigerator. And as the poet takes on the words for his own creative use in a poem he has to perform a difficult and unenviable dual task: to wrench a word out of commonality into uniqueness and at the same time to invest its uniqueness with the recognisable aura of commonality. The poem has to be thus an ambivalence: on one hand it is the most secret and charmed document of the creator's soul, and on the other it is the possession of a community to whom he gifts it. It has to be unique as well as universal, most intensely and secretly confessional and through participation and access communitarian.

The consequent tension that is generated is unique to literary and more particularly poetic creativity. If things and objects lean on their names, the names also can have no reality or significance minus the things or objects on whom they are etched. Man and his world are inseparable from the words. Ideologies that are products of history are served by words and acquire their meaning only in their servitude to history. They take birth and die like men. But the poet's ultimate dream remains to create an image through words that is non-ideological, non-historical, totally nascent and new. That is a challenge and a complicated problem.

The problem is compounded by the poet's recognition that the words cannot fully express reality. But human reality, if it is to be given shape, can be given a shape only through words.

Marshall Urban refers to the tripartite function of words. Firstly words indicate or designate, they are names. Secondly, they can also be an instinctive and spontaneous response to psychic or physical stimuli and in that form devoid of any hidden meanings and nuances. Thirdly, and most importantly, they can also be symbols and signs. Thus, in its essence language is the representation of one element of experience with the help of another. It is in Urban's words,

> the bipolar relation between the sign or the symbol and the thing signified or symbolised, and the consciousness of that relation.

This then is the basic distinction between the poet and the visual artist and the musician facing *parampara*, history or tradition. For the poet his tools, his mechanics of being himself and intuiting experience are all historical, usage-worn, anchored in the life of the group, the community. His job is to transform, reinvigorate words into new nuances and significances, into verbal flowers on the wasteland of worn out, rusted, tired social discourse. He never enjoys the benefit of his basic tools being available in their nascent, original, vibrant form. This is both an inheritance, an opportunity and also a challenge. The poet's struggle is how to be totally himself, uniquely alone and at the same time accessible to the group. A poem, and with it therefore the words constituting it and their configurations, is an attempt to transcend language, the language of everyday speech, partaking of history with its ideologies, thoughts and ideas of the social group. This social language is sought to be concentrated in the poem, given vibrancy and articulation and then raised to a heightened level of meaning and significance. That is the task of poetic creativity and its ambivalent relationship with *parampara* or tradition. In Octavio Paz's words

> the poem is language standing erect; when language is poetry each word conceals a certain metaphorical charge that is ready to explode as soon as the secret mechanism is tripped, but the creative force of the word resides in the man who utters it.

Social language is constantly being degraded. It is susceptible to such degradation by the compulsion of functional advantage. The degradation is by making it a set of dried-up and dead jargons and abstract counters bereft of meaning and hence incapable of communicating the faint whispers of the soul. This is the reason why the poet is constantly in an ambivalent relationship with the tradition which, as he is no doubt aware, defines his essential togetherness with others, the group and the community but which, unfortunately, so degrades the word that it is no longer the nascent, the pure carrier of life and reality. And his never-dying dream is to convey the latter in its true essence.

In India we would not be what we are without Vyasa and Valmiki. Their works are a mediation between society and that which both establishes it and celebrates it. Words in a poem, whether in these epics or in the best that is being written today, are revelations. They reveal to us what we are and invoke the god's blessings that man becomes what he essentially is and not what the degraded social usage of the word tells him he is.

The poet seeks to transcend the ambivalance by working out an upward movement for the words – from the language of commonality to that of poetry; from a wasteland of jargons to the dense forest of words in their sparkling shape and form. It is the loneliness of one who struggles to make the tradition, the history, the commonality unique and, through that alone, universal and not through any demographic jugglery or magic act of numbers.

On each occasion when we are served by words by using them with opportunism we are injuring them, mutilating them. The poet is not served by words. He is servant to the words; he wants to return them to the fecundity and plenitude which is their true nature, their essential Being. It is an attempt to enable them to recover this true Being and to reconquer their original state.

The poetic instant is never frozen in time. It is an instant that is for ever available in the flow of time. That is why the true poetic experience grounded in intuition denies and extols tradition in the same breath. Even while seeking to anchor words with their uniqueness into a commonality it seeks to save them from the degradation of motivated uses and jargon-making. That in essence, is the ambivalent relationship of the poetic process with *parampara*, history and tradition.

7

Parampara and the Individual

Ramesh Chandra Shah

A LOOK at the background paper provided for this seminar makes one wonder; how is it that the word 'tradition' is found so dispensable even as the word 'individual' is allowed to stand as it is? Apparently we do not feel uncomfortable with the individual as such: the concept as well as the value pertaining to this word is not perceived as something alien or disruptive. It is not uncommon, however, to hear people say that the accent on individuality or personality forms no essential part of Indian culture as it certainly does in the case of European culture: the scant respect or concern shown for the value of privacy in the Indian milieu is often seen to be an indicator of our low valuation of individuality itself. For us, it is said, 'connectedness' is the higher value: connectedness not only with the other human beings in ever-widening circles of family, community, village, country and, ultimately, with the whole of humanity, but also with the sub-human as well as super human orders of creation. But, does this necessarily reduce or frustrate individuality? Ideally, the invitation and realisation of one's connectedness in the universe ought to enrich and fortify rather they confuse or obstruct the full flowering of an individual. Realistically, however, since no civilisation can fully realise its foundational principles — human nature being what it is — and since every *parampara* is bound to face periods of decline (*dharmaglani*) owing to internal or external factors, problems may arise; conventional rigidities may put too much strain upon the individual. Contact or encounter with other cultures, then, may produce beneficial as well as baneful results. By facilitating and fostering the growth of individuality as well as self-assertion, such encounters may either lead to self-awareness of the sort that recharges and renews the springs of *parampara* itself through the awakened individual; or by unleashing the energies of freedom without responsibility, by releasing the individual from all the restraints imposed on his instincts of aggression and acquisition by the traditional obligations of connectedness, such cultural changes may induce the worst kind of individualism — such as we are witnessing today in our own milieu. Had not Jaishankar Prasad in his epic poem *Kamayani* warned us long ago?

> *apane mein sab kuchh bhar kaise*
> *vyakti vikas karega*
>
> *yaha ekanta svartha bhishan hai .*
> *apana nash karega*

That is exactly the *paramparika* wisdom voiced by the poet here; it is egocentric and unrestrained individualism, that is the worst enemy of the individual himself because it works against the best interest of his own higher self. It is suicidal, because it kills the very possibilities of self-realisation, that is, of real fulfilment. Are not these lines a reassertion and restatement in contemporary terms of what the poet of the *Bhagavad Gita* had sung long ago: *atma hi atmano bandhuh, atmaiva ripuratmanah*? And it is no mere coincidence that the most realistic and terrifying clear insight into the nature of the relationship between the gifted or privileged individuals on the one hand and the rest of the society on the other, has also been recorded in the same text: *yadyadacharati sreshthah, tattadevetard janah/sa yatpramanam kurute, lokastadanuvartate* ['Whatever a great man does, people will imitate; they follow his example'.] That is exactly the way a *parampara* is maintained and transmitted; and that is also the way it disintegrates and declines. The role of the privileged individual, or, by implication — the role of a group of privileged individuals, called the intelligentsia in the Western world — is thus defined and delineated here in the most unambiguous terms.

Vyashti and *samashti* are our traditional equivalents for the individual and the collective. But *samashti* comprehends much more than the human collective of a monocentred universe: it comprehends the whole of creation — *charachara srishti*. *Vyasthi*, on the other hand, somehow does not seem to convey all that is sought to be conveyed by terms like the individual or person. Western culture seems to be much more sophisticated on that acccount; and, therefore, the word *vyakta* as the equivalent for the individual and the word *vyaktitva* as the equivalent for individuality or personality are probably later coinages to meet the requirements of a new age and new sensibility. *Vyakti* perhaps literally means manifestation. Adding the prefix *abhi*, — we get *abhivyakti* which, again, is expression or manifestation.Thus, the coinage, even as coinage has a certain metaphysical resonance and validity. In chapter ten of the *Bhagavad Gita* called *Vibhuti-yoga*, we hear Krishna telling Arjuna:

> there is no limit to my divine manifestations; whatever in this world is powerful, beautiful or glorious has come forth from a fruitition of my power and glory.

Here it would be pertinent to remember that even in common speech a great personality or *mahapurusha* is characterised as *vibhut* — exactly in the sense which the *Gita* gives to this word, as if what constitutes the greatness or the uniqueness of an individual has nothing to do with the individual as such: it is the radiance through him of something supra-individual, mysterious or divine. Since it sounds a little bit premature to bring in association of religion or spirituality into a conversation focused on tradition and individuality, let me have recourse to my own securely secular field of literature.

2

Way back during the forties, Agyeya — the leader of the modernist movement in Hindi poetry — seeking an ally in T.S. Eliot, had Hindi-ised his famous essay called 'Tradition and Individual Talent'. It was a freely attempted creative adaptation rather than a literal rendering and he chose to call it *rurhi aur maulikata*, instead of *parampara* aur *vyakti-pratibha*. Of course, Eliot's use of the word 'tradition' was closer to what we mean by our *parampara*, as Agyeya could very well perceive; but he also knew that *parampara* as such was not inimical, but conducive to and inclusive of the gifted individual in the creative enterprise of civilisation. Eliot's 'tradition' was an ideal 'construct'; he saw the values of European culture threatened from within itself and sought an ally in Eastern *parampara*. The existential situation for the Indian poet was different: here the threat came primarily from without, but also from within. Here it was *Rurhi* — that is, tradition become congealed and counter-productive through a long dependence on defence-mechanisms and the consequent emaciation of creative and affirmative capabilities. Whereas Western civilisational values were threatened by the consequences of its own over-adventurism — by its own calculative enterprise of conceptual control of the universe, Indian culture, on the other hand, seemed to be threatened by its inertia and loss of creative self-confidence. Eliot had sought to upgrade his 'tradition' and, therefore, to present it in the garb of *parampara* – availing himself of the insights he had gained from the exposure of his sensibility to Indian metaphysics and poetry. Agyeya, his Hindi counterpart on the other hand, needed the other corrective for a revitalisation of the metaphysically sound but creatively almost exhausted *parampara*. That is why he chose to upgrade individuality as *maulikata* – as the principle of creative innovation and adventure, that is why he substituted *rurhi* for Eliot's tradition, because what he had to contend with and overcome was the obstacle of *rurhi* and not *parampara* as such. One recalls his insistence on search for individuality (*vyaktitva ki khoja*) on the one hand and on the necessity to build up a nation of critics (*alochaka rashtra ka nirmana*) on the other hand: both were part of a poet's dream of self-regeneration through cultural reconstruction. 'In dreams begin responsibilities' – as W.B. Yeats had said.

It looks as if the disease which afflicted the Western cultural enterprise particularly since the Renaissance is what we using our own ancestral terminology, could diagnose as an over-activity of *rajoguna*, while the problem that had come to plague our own civilisation was a weakening of the *rajas* and a preponderance of *tamas.* That this rather simplistic-looking picture is not altogether tame can be demonstrated by the facts that stare us in the face today everywhere around us. It was *Rurhi* – tradition hardened and congealed into a mere mechanism of defensive sensibility – which had been responsible for the over-all stagnation of Indian life and thought in the post-medieval periods. It had resulted in what Sri. Aurobindo in his 'The Life Divine' has rightly characterised as a 'great poverty of life'. Contact with the vital West with its accent on the state and the individual as well as its great capacity for the organisation of resources was bound to have an impact which had its sunny as well as shadowy side. The brighter side is reflected in the successful adoption of many Western ideas and institutions as well as in the consequent catalysation of our own native capacities. The shadowy side was evident in what the philosopher K.C. Bhattacharya could perceive as far back as 1929, as the phenomenon of shadow-mind resistance to what he himself calls '*svaraj* in ideas' and in what Mahatma Gandhi characterised as 'our hard-hearted intelligentsia' and as 'the longest nightmare of my life'. We can detect the same evil today all around us in the peculiar virulence with which the virus of politicisation of everything has come to infect every aspect of our national life and also in the unprecedented corruption of long-suppressed instincts of aggression and acquisition. Just as the individual had come to be overshadowed and thwarted by tradition congealed into *rurhi*, over-activation of the same through a confusedly permissive and value-blind (*mulya-marh*) milieu has made him reserve his own interests at the cost of community and country. *Rurhi* has been loosened and even discarded; but the new-found freedom of the individual — initially productive — has now become counter-productive. It certainly hasn't contributed much towards the revitalisation of *parampara*, as was expected from it.

Nevertheless, it is worth mentioning that even a most consistently negativistic critic like V.S. Naipaul, who so far had seen nothing in Indian spiritual tradition except the most insidious enemy of the Western and modernist ideals of progress and organisational energy, has suddenly adopted a more optimistic and positive attitude. In his latest book called *India: a million mutinies now*, he seems to have come to the conclusion that the much-maligned passivity and question of Indian tradition is resilient enough to absorb new ideas, to accept challenges and even to master science and technology in its own way.

3

As the example of Eliot alone from the literary West would appear to indicate, tradition itself was a discovery — or, a re-discovery — of the modern mind. It was the mind which could define and articulate its own tragedy in terms of what it chose to call 'the disinherited mind'. That is the kind of painful self-knowledge which enabled it to realise the significance of Goethe's desperate quarrel with Newton on the one hand and the hollowness at the heart of the doomsday rhetoric of Spengler on the other hand. That was the kind of self-knowledge which could produce poets like Rilke and Holderline who sang of the departed gods and the homelessness of modern man. That's what enabled W.B. Yeats to take seriously

> the central experience of Indian civilisation — that experience, wherein all thoughts and all emotions expect their satisfaction and rest.

If modernity could thus be looked upon as the homelessness of modern man, *parampara* or the voice of the sacred would present itself as that home for which the modern man has been searching. It was the self-religion of the self, about which Yeats, quoting *Chandogya Upanishad*, says: 'the wise man sees in self those that are alive and those that are dead'. One recalls at this juncture the opening verses of chapter IV of the *Gita*, which, to my mind, constitutes a quintessential account of *parampara* itself: 'Now I have shown you' — Krishna says, '*Yoga* that leads to the truth undying. I taught this yoga first to Vivasvat, Vivasvat taught it in turn to Manu. Next Ikshvaku learnt it from Manu, and so the sages in royal succession carried it onward from teacher to teacher, till at length it was lost, throughout ages, forgotten.'

Is it not strange that the wisdom of *parampara* should thus acknowledge its own vulnerability to the destructive power of time: *sa kaleneha muhala yogo nashtah parantapa*? But, it is the nature of wisdom to be illusion-proof and clear-sighted. It does not claim immortality for itself, but for that from which it emanates. Immediately after this inevitable loss of *parampara* and collective amnesia has been acknowledged, the time-bound human consciousness of Arjuna is filled with doubt: 'Vivasvat was born long before you. How am I to believe that-you were the first to teach this *yoga*? 'Krishna's answer not only subsumes 'the wise man' of the *Chandogya Upanishad*, 'who sees in self those that are alive and those that are dead', but also illumines the way *parampara* resurrects itself through an incarnation of that very self:

> You and I, Arjuna
> Have lived many lives.
>
> I remember them all:
> You do not remember . . . .
>
> When goodness grows weak
> When evil increases
> I make myself a body.
>
> In every age I come back
> To deliver the holy
> To destroy the sin of the sinner
> To establish righteousness.

Parampara is thus linked to what W.B. Yeats has called 'the great memory'. He ascribes this 'age-long memorised self' (his own phrase) not only to man but to bird and beast alike — because they too are the living symbols of the divine order, the *rita*, glimpsed by inspired sages and their reverent listeners. They have not been created merely for the consumption of man as some historical traditions would have us believe.

4

Are we now in a position to confront the issues raised in the background paper? What is the source of *parampara*, it asks. Well, the same age-long memorised self, which operates through bird and beast and man alike but achieves self-consciousness in man. How does it flow in time? Through the channels of interconnected selves, each of which is self-contained, and yet, potentially a self-transcending unit of the whole. Who possesses it? Of course, the individual self or *jivatman* who is sufficiently illuminated through intuition or discipline to realise that Unity of Being which all civilisations, all religions and artistic endeavours have aspired to. Yes, it is a knowledge system, a metaphysics, a religion of the self; but also a praxis, a *sadhana*. Does it hold in potential the characteristics of all orders of knowledge? Yes, it would seem that by dint of its experiential access to the divine order of things, and to the creative reconciliation of opposites in the unity of being, it has the in-built capacity to connect and co-ordinate all orders of knowledge.

Is an individual the parent of the primal seed of *parampara*? Yes and no. Is Bharata or Vyasa the name of an individual or of a succession of sages, their minds and voices! But what about Kalidasa, Tulsidasa and Jaideva? What about Ramakrishna Paramhamsa, Aurobindo and Ramana Maharishi? They certainly were luminous individual centres radiating *parampara* like its authentic source itself. *Parampara* does seem to revolve around meditation and meditative thinking and, in fact, on what is called *yoga*. Heidegger in his critique of the history of Western philosophy has demonstrated how this tradition deviated into an objective and calculative direction and how nuclear fission was the logical culmination of this calculative thinking. The background paper has also drawn our attention to the conditions under which individualism rather than individuality becomes the normative principle. How to restore the equilibrium? — that is the question and the way to answer this question automatically leads us to another question which too has been raised in the paper itself:

> What is the experience of the self where the duality between subject and object is lost and the individual artist becomes

empowered to transmit the quintessence of a *parampara* in ever-renewing forms of contemporary relevance?

The answer, it seems, is contained in the question itself, because it appeals to that highest common factor of all religions, that perennial philosophy or *sanatana dharma*, which has always and everywhere been the metaphysical system of the prophets, saints and sages. As Aldous Huxley in his beautiful introduction to a translation of the *Bhagavad Gita* says,

> It is only in the act of contemplation, when words and even personality are transcended, that the pure state of the perennial Philosophy can actually be known. The records left by those who have known it in this way make it abundantly clear that all of them, whether Hindu, Buddhist, Hebrew, Taoist, Christian or Mohammedan, were attempting to describe the same essentially indescribable fact.

That indeed is the source of *parampara*. But the struggle of the individual towards this *paramparika* wisdom — the live process as well as attainment — is nowhere better exemplified than in the work of the artists and the poets. It's this kind of internal evidence that speaks directly to us in our confusion and distress, because it's the poet, the artist, who shares not only our aspirations to Unity of Being, but also our fragmented existential condition.

> Labour is blossoming or dancing where,
> The body is not bruised to pleasure soul,
> Nor beauty born out of its own despair,
> Nor blear-eyed wisdom out of midnight oil.
>
> O chestnut tree, great-rooted blossomer
> Are you the leaf, the blossom or the bole?
> O body swayed to music, O brightening glance,
> How can we know the dancer from the dance?

8

Parampara and the Individual: Beyond Duality

S.C. Malik

Introduction

HUMANISM in the sense of man's power and glory has dominated modern man for almost 500 years, spreading from Europe everywhere, transforming life through a mechanical and fragmentary approach, especially its belief in the full dominion over nature through industrialisation. It was hoped that the flowering of full human potential and creativity would be the result of this ushering in of radical humanism which begins with the Age of Enlightenment. Never before in human history has all of humanity been made aware of its individual rights at all levels. Never before have so many resources been available for all levels of society, for everyone through the modernisation processes, not ideally but actually. These positive aspects need to be remembered since notions of equal human dignity and brotherhood have always been talked about but the means of production in such a large scale were seldom possible earlier because wealth and power were generally cornered by a few, nor were the means for mass production available. Relatively speaking, and at a global scale, this remains true in any case. But the ascendancy of these notions, linked with Euro-American domination and its affluent life-style which everyone obviously wants to copy, is also a history drowned in blood, indignity, and injustice. Unfortunately, the original maxims of humanism with centrality of perennial values has been replaced by modern social goals of maximum economic profit through mass production and consumerism. It has led to mindless frivolity, addiction and passivity. This latter aspect of humanism, devoid of the sacred, has led to ecological degradation, breakdown of social networks and families that held together a civil society through some moral — cosmic — world-views and values. (Lane, 1996)

Tradition and modernity

Speaking of tradition implies the context of modernity. Social scientists no longer see these as referring to confrontational concepts. Tradition and modernity do not refer to definite, internally consistent and mutually exclusive entities as considered by some. The unreflective use of these terms has only led to dire results, because these terms are equated with crucial variables, i.e., agrarian *versus* industrial society, authority *versus* freedom, scientific *versus* prescientific mentality and so on. But the function of these terms depends upon the context, and whichever variable is considered crucial. There is no inherent incompatibility between the two, unless tradition is considered to be a static setting whose essential features are described in terms of few well-chosen propositions. It may be that often traditions appear in new garbs, that in traditional societies diachronic changes did take place. On the other hand, modernity is equated with change as a value but it may be only within the established order, i.e., the talk of futurology, particularly technology, is for the most part based on the extrapolation of certain variables which are regarded as established and irreversible. In many ways, modernity is very conservative as some variables are regarded as an inexorable fixity. For example, the notion that tradition is often homogeneous, and often conceptualised in a fixed dogma — either simple or very complicated; seen within simple categories of folk/village/tribal societies without much internal differentiation. Of course, tradition or notions about the past are also used for modernising societies in terms of choosing from traditional modalities of thought, attitudes and sensibilities. If the same traditional societies are also thought to be comprising closed symbolic systems limited to a particular strata of high culture, precisely the same may be said about modern elites — intellectual and academics — who are hardly accessible to the man in the street. But in traditional societies, sayings of great leaders, saints, is often available to the masses in a great deal more ways for centuries, than our own leaders whose memory may last for not more than a couple of decades.

Thus, tradition cannot be reduced to some simple integrated system, like modernisation, unless it is equated with Westernisation. Nor is it logically true that liberty, equality and democracy cannot take place without modernisation — without this obsessive concern with economic growth; the latter in fact may often lead to totalitarian tendencies or the hegemony of one style of socio-economic and political life wherein the anthropocentric and technocentric world-view is inhuman, meaningless and valueless. Nevertheless, the tension and conflicts are there in modernity too, since it is far from any kind of completed or synthetic whole. The history of the modern period is not simply the record of intellectual expansion and material growth, since science and technology have been gravely misused by its creators for war and mass murder; it does not reflect the original scientific confidence of the secular humanist — in fact there is increase in human despair and nihilism. (Eisanstadt and Gramherd, 1973)

On the other hand, strong traditions persist in modern or modernising societies. It is well known that traditional knowledge is used by groups or forces — caste or other groups — in order to reorganise themselves in new modern setting in effective ways with hegemony in metropolitan centres. In traditional societies there is an allowance for a constant redefinition and recrystallisation, although restriction of the distribution of wealth and power often does not allow for too much free creative activity. This is true for modernity also, wherein there is hostility towards the very act of creativity and self-expression. (Malik, 1978, 1987a)

The Individual and Cultural Identity

The goals of universal prosperity have led today to a loss of not only cultural landscape but also to a sense of well-being of the individual, to his alienation and disorientation. Contradictorily, this is despite the fact of giving so much importance and significance to the individual who is central to the entire context of 'progress'. Because there is loss of identity, there are new collective attempts to seek socio-political and ethnic identities that are causing conflicts all around the globe. The individual is at a loss, since he/she has almost completely lost any notion of authenticity and creativity. The futility of personal and collective lives, and the aimlessness and meaning of life which is causing suffering is all too obvious. This is a general neurosis of this age, not only at the socio-psychological level but because modern civilisation is no longer in touch with our — humankind's — million year-old archetypal natures that is crucial to mental health and emotional well-being. (Malik, 1995a)

The general lack of creative and imaginative possibilities needs to be addressed by resurrecting such possibilities and this is closely linked to a radical transformation in the consciousness of man. This is the cultural evolution, of creating new perspectives and visions, which has begun in some sense in the linking of contemporary science and ancient wisdom. But this change is limited to a minority.

For the moment, there is no need to historically trace these various developments, as is well known about what happened in this modern deviation from the end of the Middle Ages in Europe and the rise of individualism, the atomistic centralisation of the little self. What needs to be pointed out is that traditional societies everywhere served powers higher than themselves — call it the mythological or some cosmic dimension which formed a part (not apart!) of the original instruction of creative symbolism, appreciating natural diversity and compelling refinement. Many of the peoples all over the world not yet overwhelmed by modernity of the European origins, the 'indigenous' peoples, are truly human. They are not inferior as has been the approach to all notions and research about non-Europeans and as modern man has been brainwashed into believing, because the criteria of 'development' in general is technology and economics. This is a false correlation as is so obvious, since the maximum flowering of aesthetic and ethical expressions of a higher order is found amongst precisely those that are at the lowest rung of the ladder in the techno-economic scale. It is all to see the expressions of urban living which is rich but ugly in all ways — aesthetic only, ethic only, on a personal level personal and where social distress is concerned; leave aside those 'living' in the slums. Living has become a matter of individual experience and appreciation rather than arising out of a 'communal' experience — in the sense of a communion between man, nature and the cosmos. So, why is the individual today lacking in creativity even though it seems obvious that the individual is the unit of this authenticity (maybe this assumption itself is false?) Isn't it possible that some erroneous fundamental assumptions are the cause of this distress, especially in the social sciences; say, of discussing such contemporary issues within contrasting terms, i.e., 'individual *versus* society'; 'modernity *versus* tradition'; 'nature *versus* man'; 'objectivity *versus* subjectivity'; 'science *versus* religion(art)'; 'individual *versus* *parampara*', and so on? (Malik, 1995c)

There are many examples which show that, before the Age of Enlightenment, creative manifest expressions in music, dance, art, architecture arose in a talented individual from a unity of being; this underlying philosophy was witnessed in everyday activities related to food, dress, ornaments, interpersonal behaviour and so on. No activity was unrelated to this idea of harmony, governed by perennial truths, changeless principles, within which social obligations and time-honoured skills were transmitted through collective patterns of universal energies. In this sense tradition was the perpetuation of knowledge systems; it was a continuous maintenance of perennial values through changing external manifestations. In short, *parampara* is a movement, a continuous change in the NOW, the past and future coalescing and emerging from the experiential present, the NOW, which is not the mere abstraction of the intellect. Tradition in this sense is not as social scientists have believed something that is static, something that stifles imagination and is a soulless repetition lacking originality especially as the individual is supposed to get lost in some socio-cultural conformity with minor deviations available to him. Maybe the individual in such traditional societies considers himself not separate (apart) but a part of an organic whole towards the harmony of which he strives; and, in this process, creates and innovates the vitality necessary for the totality, acting as mediator between the divine and the social set-up. For him/her the entire universe is all that is sacred in any case! For example, in traditional cultures, there is no such thing as 'art' in the reified sense of the word: 'art' is specifically in the service of, or incorporated into the religious life of, the civilisation or culture, and this religious life is a seamless totality which incorporates every aspect of existence. In contrast, the post-Renaissance concept of Art is laden with assumptions for which there are no non-Human equivalents. This is Art for Art's sake, characterised by loftiness and unapproachability, unlike 'art' which is closely interwoven with the activities of everyday life. (Malik *et. al*, 1994, 1995b)

What kind of Knowledge?

The question that may be asked in the context of *parampara* is, how is all this knowledge, of various kinds, transmitted? The answer has been sought in various ways in the social sciences and there are many explanations of this in traditional sources. The reference in this paper is to another kind of knowledge which needs to be emphasised, since the distinction between different systems of knowledge is crucial to our understanding of the theme, and this is not clear at all. Knowledge is of many levels and differs drastically in the qualitative sense. Briefly, this argument may be stated as follows. One important source of knowledge arises out of a universal dimension wherein lies creativity, happiness, cultural imagination and the like; all these categories are the prerogative of all beings without being linked to any specific structural notion. It is related to matters of the heart and not isolated in the head. When the latter ignores the psychic function of transcendence, culture becomes aberrant because harmony cannot be realised solely by intellectual rationality. (Malik, 1996, 1997)

The sense of the sacred is the function of this cosmic mystery of existence which permeates all of the universe, giving a sense of awe, reverence and beauty — being the *sinequanon* for creativity and authenticity. The source of this knowledge lies in another realm and dimension, and transcendence is to be located not elsewhere but in the 'present', in the NOW only; in daily life, in the so-called mundane which is a reflection of the cosmic dimension. In short, creativity is a process, not an end product; it is an intention when the head and the heart go together rather than the result which is crucial for this way of life. (Malik, 1993).

Post-Renaissance Knowledge-systems and the Emergence of Dichotomies

Each age and culture conducts its life from its own insights into the mysteries of reality and each belief system; philosophy of life shapes its peoples in terms of their place in the cosmos, not primarily in terms of what it knows but what it believes in. However, since the domination of the sixteenth-seventeenth century Europe true reality was valued in sensory perception; developing into the well-known paradigms, Cartesian, Newtonian, Mechanical, and Scientific. In its wake it brought in astonishing analytical procedures and with it gains which are indisputable because superstition, ignorance, domination of the church, etc., were left behind in favour of rational thought. Mind and matter were thus seen as separate entities with cerebral consciousness as the only principle to grasp reality, at the expense of the indivisibility (individual means indivisible as one dictionary meaning) of the being. Resultantly, these partial approaches fragmented the complex unity of human nature and culture. (Malik, 1989a, b).

The head and the heart separation was to continue for another 500 years, between conscious and the unconscious, object and subject, values and thought, between instinct and reason, between Art and technics, etc. It was to induce a schizoid attitude of mind and culture, wherein it was not cosmic order but quantitative science which dictated life. Everything has been affected by this attitude in the modern world. Not that there were not any protests against all these developments, but this is not the place to discuss those.

Along with these developments what is important to note is that in the fifteenth century grew the germ of individuality, in opposition to the domination of the clergy, theology and nobility. A new faith in human omnipotence was the source of this new sense of individual personality, attaining in time a superhuman status with unlimited possibilities. Of course, there is the obvious bright side to these microcosmic expressions of humanism.

In the history of human civilization, the disappearance of the archetypal and the universal, to be replaced by the particular individual, happened for the first time on such a large scale — as part of the assumption of human control. But this meant the separation of the 'inside' from the 'outside' within the individual; the emergence of personal autonomy, a sense of independence from the family, religious and social beliefs, from obligations, from oppressive political and social structures — in short from community and society itself. Needless to say, with this very freedom, it has in our times brought about alienation, the search for all kinds of identities, a sense of meaninglessness. The search has begun to come full circle since the social sciences — the sciences and all — are speaking of interrelatendness, holistic searches and what not. Nevertheless, it is still in the external world where the search is on, and nowhere near does it take into account the heart, intuition and experiential dimension as its crucial source of knowledge. The split between the sacred and the secular continues.

In this overall view of culture, material values become paramount, associated with the 'real' individual who believes in the omnipotence of wealth, and the concommitant values which satisfy man's psychological needs and material comfort; hence the convergence of open market and private ownership. It speaks of private spaces; and it is reflected in contemporary art forms, architecture, furniture, literature, printed word and literacy and private means of communication. These are all part of the developments of the private personal self. What it lacks are the magical moments, an increasing neglect of the eternal — perennial — values, which have come to be replaced by temporary, or short-lived considerations.

Today individualism and human control is taken for granted; it is ubiquitous and unquestioned. The destruction and atomisation of human communities on a global scale, of the psyche is now complete. It also means the complete hegemony of the masculine, essentially egotistical and the secularist; as opposed to the feminine, integrated and interrelatedness that relies on the basis of sharing and co-operation. Spiritual isolation is characteristic of industrialisation which the developing world is following suit very rapidly; this value is one of bondage to calculation, routine, and utilitarian education which has made individuals into mind-machines.

Transmission of Traditional Knowledge-systems and Modernity

Before writing, and before the printed word came into existence, learning took place in many ways, and knowledge was passed on rather rigourously from one generation to the next. In this passing on of *parampara* — tradition — it was the parents, teachers and the older members of the community who played a crucial role. This direct passing on is not at a premium in the modern world where books, television, radio, cinema and other forms of modern communications including frequent travelling are major resource inputs. In short, today, knowledge is passed on through impersonal means so that much of both relevant and irrelevant information is given to a mass of individuals. There was the written word earlier too, but it was not easily accessible for the many, nor was it meant for the masses. In India, it was only from the nineteenth century onwards that the printed word began to bring about a modern manner of cultural transformation in the country — a major way of organising knowledge and culture. (Wood, 1985).

Prior to all these modern developments, learning was a process located under a large holistic umbrella in which living was part of absorbing knowledge, not separated and fragmented as we find later on and today. The direct personal contact through the extended family (it is not the nuclear bomb which is a threat at the socio-cultural level but the nuclear family that has also caused a horrendous catastrophe which is worse than the bomb in many ways), village community, and also through carefully trained teachers with whom learning was also personal; all these networks formed the totality within which creativity — culture and knowledge-systems — was transmitted, call it 'folk', 'tribal' or 'classic', i.e., classificatory schemes which hold little water in the situation of Indian civilisation. (Malik, 1968, 1971, 1975)

The passing on of culture in this manner also requires that society be geared to specific cultural forms whether these be tools or techniques, emotional symbols of value, intellectual concepts or theories. These forms have to be remembered in traditional societies by all its members, and this is why specific forms (like rituals) are not to be forgotten, as we are able to do today, easily as living forms.

Even though much of such knowledge is being recorded and form a data-base for research, and it may be reproduced at any time, this recall is in a dead memory way. Therefore, earlier in traditional communities (pre-modern times), more accuracy was required, ensuring that details of form were correctly maintained, and intensively. Life was thus organised formally and intensively, not extensively as today, in order that reproduction is passed in great detail as part of a live culture, i.e., ceremonies, rituals, customs and conventions, intellectual learning; all this was carried through repetition and concentration until it became a part of one's life, thus to gain mastery over life through this manner of observation, repetition, and concentration which allowed one to do difficult things as if spontaneously. (Wood, 1985).

In all this traditional social order, faith and obedience become important in such rigorous training, implying that self-restraint and authority were emphasised, not individuality and freedom of the lower self, or lower self-expression, so that conformity to norms and values was strictly adhered to even if the eventual goal was 'personal' *moksha*. But this seemingly dictatorial attitude from the modern viewpoint was possible because here was an ingrained attitude of respect and reverence towards those who were repositories of traditional knowledge, and in whose heads it was stored and passed on through tightly organised systems of condensed forms, from person to person. This is where the notion of the sacred comes in since these are sanctioned through symbols, rituals, ceremonies which are to be respected. It is spiritual reverence which ultimately governed social and cultural behaviour requiring an organisational principle of hierarchy of values and social positions. (Malik, 1977, 1987b)

Today, there are seldom any moral — ethical and aesthetic — values as inclusive (intrinsic or extrinsic) that give a backing to the modern-day law-givers. Moreover, today equality is taken literally, and independence of the mind and secularism is emphasised since religion and matters of spirit are of individual choice. But the modern way, in which personal contact is a social and cultural setting of learning, is missing. Alienation and isolation of so-called free-thinking individual has reached its limits in mass destruction since one no longer feels related to other beings, to nature, to the earth, to the universe even though the organism knows it to be otherwise. The psychological consequences of this order of modern individual's isolation is the evidence of increasing mental diseases.

There is little need to elaborate the exact means of the traditional manner of transmission of values as this is well known. To name a few, temples, pilgrimage centres where the art and architecture reminded one of many other aspects of life; then the teachers, families, and so on. In short, strict means of transmitting knowledge existed — be it practical, emotional or intellectual. But in all of this the individual had to be subservient psychologically to larger units which gave authenticity, power and authority in terms of appropriate rituals at every step so that the overall cover of faith, obedience, reverence was adhered to; in the absence of which this learning was useless. There was direct personal contact (not personal in the modern context since it is not a romantic emotional relationship but the transmission through strict codified laws, both cultural and hence social, since select groups would specialise in one area or the other — akin to the distribution of work that is a function of a totality spatially and temporally within which each individual is born already; it is a given situation, a matrix of existence affecting each member simultaneously) that mentally transforms the individual, unlike today where sequential steps — from intellectual, emotional and practical — are to be followed. The modern way is called reason and logic, whereas the former is called superstition, ignorance and irrationality. (Malik, 1968, 1971)

In traditional societies, since the 'sacred' was the covering umbrella, there was no separation between the body and the mind, the self and tradition or society, between nature and man, and man and the universe. In short, each individual functioned within this overarching world-view, learnt largely through 'unsaid' means of communication. There was a traditional philosophy of life that governed all of life and not any specialised area; it was applicable to all areas of life and experience of reality, i.e., there existed certain ultimate principles, perennial laws, and values which governed all of existence. Hence, through time, while cultural forms and symbols, tools and techniques changed, some essence of knowledge continued, allowing for the transmission of tradition at the emotional, intellectual and practical level. But when this essence of the 'being of a civilisation' is lost and knowledge in this sense is not there then, as today, knowledge remains only at the informative, quantitative and empirical level.

Thus, in the absence of another order — the source from which all else is generated in the phenomenal world, when this is given up, then *parampara* remains at the superficial level, in fact its end is near. Needless to add, it is possible for anyone to misuse any technique, ritual and modern idea of freedom to extreme negative ends. But that does not prove the efficacy or inefficacy of a specific thing or concept (for example, a pen could also be used for stabbing. (Malik, 1990a, b, c)

Summing up

This paper is in response to the preamble sent by the organisers about this seminar. Presumably there could be several reasons for discussing this theme: the imperatives of our times, its confusions and the consequent misdirections or directions that India is especially moving towards. Aren't these attempts by humanity, to seek and grope in the dark for answers, because of the serious contemporary crisis of modern civilisation? But in this process is it sound to project another unattainable utopia in the twenty-first century? Clearly, the theme needs to be contextualised both in general terms and specifically for the Indian scenario, and even if it is a mere philosophical issue can it exist in a vacuum? Isn't it important that certain basic assumptions which underlie the theme, along with terms and definitions be given our attention both philosophically and culture-historically? For instance, are the individual and *parampara* as two separate categories appropriate even in terms of mere operational purposes? Is it possible that the modern world is in such a predicament because it operates within certain outdated confrontational dualities which are essentially false and irrelevant and therefore the confusion and misdirection arises? Say, like the son of a barren women, the existence of the sky, and even in terms of science which presumes that the universe consists of separate objects which need to be comprehended within some unified theoretical system of knowledge? Isn't it possible that it is all one, and that it is more pertinent to ask why we see this separation, this duality? It is like assuming that there is a thinker separate from thought, which is common knowledge, but is it true? Or, is it accurate to ask a question whether the drop is separate from the ocean, and isn't it possible that not only does the ocean contain drops but also that the drop is the ocean? Isn't it possible that if we move beyond this basic paradigm of dualities, the directions will be clearer? Moreover, speaking of *parampara* or tradition, doesn't it become essential to contextualise the theme within the many notions of modernity? It is to these and related issues that this paper has addressed itself even though so briefly.

References

Eisenstadt, S.N. and Graubard, S.R., 1973, *Intellectuals and Tradition*, New York, Humanities Press.

Lane, John, 1966, *A Snake's Tail Full of Ants, Art, Ecology and Consciousness*, A Resurgence Book.

Malik, S.C., 1968, *Indian Civilization; the Formative Period — A Study of Archaeology as Anthropology*, Shimla (reprinted, 1987).

———, (ed.), 1971, *Indian Civilization: The First Phase— Problems of a Source book*, Shimla.

———, 1975, *Understanding Indian Civilization - A Framework of Enquiry*, Shimla.

———, 1977, *Dissent, Protest and Reform Movements in Indian Civilization*, Shimla (ed.), IIAS.

———, 1978, 'Indian Civilization: New Images of the Past for a Developing Nation, in *The New Wind — Changing Identities*, The Hague.

———, 1987a, 'Tradition, Development and Modernity — Some Reflections, *Man in India*.

———, 1987b, *Determinants of Social Status in India*, Shimla. (ed.) IIAS.

———, 1989a, *Modern Civilization — A Crisis of Fragmentation*, New Delhi.

———, 1989b, 'Intellectuals, Traditions and Ethnographic Studies — some basic questions', *Man in India*, Ranchi.

———, 1990a, 'Holism and Life-style Studies — The Civilizational Context, *The Eastern Anthropologist*.

———, 1990b, 'Shifting Paradigm of Identity: from Becoming to Being', *Tata Institute of Social Science Journal*, Bombay.

———, 1990c, *In search of Quality of Life in Anthropology: 'Beyond Fragmentation*, Shimla.

Malik, S.C., 1994, (ed. with Saraswati, B.N. and Khanna, Madhu), *Art: The Integral Vision*, New Delhi, D.K. Printworld.

———, 1995a, *Reconceptualising the Sciences and the Humanities, An Integral Approach*, Manohar.

———, 1995b, *Inter-Cultural Dialogue and the Human Image*, (ed.) Maurice Friedman, New Delhi, IGNCA.

———, 1995c, *Touchstones of Experience: Rethinking Cultural Information Models*, New Delhi, IGNCA.

———, 1996, 'Dynamics of Cultural Communication — Rita and the *'Anthropology of Experience'*, New Delhi, IGNCA.

———, 1997, *'Now — A Dimensionless (No-Mind Sunya) State*,New Delhi,IGNCA.

Wood, Ananda, 1985, *Knowledge Before Printing and After — The Indian Tradition in Changing Kerala*, OUP.

9

The Individual and the Indian Spiritual Tradition

M.M. Agrawal

EVER since the beginning of modernity, the new Age of Reason, we have witnessed a steady growth of experimental science, capitalistic economy and, alongside with it, an overpowering cult of Individualism developing into almost a social ideology. Unfortunately, however, individualism as an ideology, with its focus on the pursuit of self-fulfilment, easily degenerates into egoistic-consumerism undermining the tradition or *parampara*. It has managed to enlarge the area of personal freedom to the extent that the individual seems to have lost all sense of social responsibility traditionally enshrined in *parampara*. In the name of 'untraditional' (a synonym for 'modern') almost anything goes — all kinds of trends, cults and styles. What sort of 'individual' does the cult of individualism presuppose? How free is the individual? What is the meaning of 'individuality'? What is the true nature of *parampara*? Is the rise of individualism necessarily incompatible with respect to tradition? Can an individual grow and realise his human potential without participation in tradition? These are some of the questions that I have tried to answer in this paper.

Individual, Individuality and Individualism

Behind contemporary individualism lies a notion of the 'self' which originating with Descartes (though he mistakenly identified it with the 'mind') has received considerable philosophical support throughout modernity. In its modified modern form it is the notion that the self is an individual mental substance, simple, indivisible, remaining constant throughout its changing biography. It is an entity which is capable of existing separately from the rest of Being including one's own body. It is no other than the essential 'I', the 'me', the subject of all my experiences. It draws the picture of the individual as a pure egoistic will inhabiting an immortal concrete substance. It is easy to see that such a conception of the self easily lends support to the idea of 'personal fulfilment' as the primary goal of life which, in its materialistic version, shades into egoistic consumerism. Are we really such kind of individuals?

In the face of the fact the *human* being, with whom we are first and foremost acquainted, both in respect of his mind and body, is constantly and unavoidably *dependent* for existence upon its immediate environment which in turn depends upon the interconnectedness of an extraordinarily complex 'whole'. It is difficult to believe that human beings are essentially ontologically separate entities. They may be islands to themselves, but we know that islands could never exist without the solid earth to support the waters that surround them. Is it then that the most widely accepted view of ourselves is mistaken; that human beings are not really separate individual entities, that the belief in such separateness is a myth promoted by the human desire for an eternal *personal* existence, which in itself is based in the fear and insecurity generated by the 'impermanence of all things'?

Surely 'the individual' as an objective reference point is an actuality. Our human *needs* — physical, psychological and spiritual — constantly refer us to a 'centre' which has to be represented as an entity separate from other similar entities. Again, the unity of consciousness in human experience constantly suggests that I am 'I' and no other thing or person. Our experience of others, though suggests an intersubjectivity, is all pervasively dualistic. Yet at no level of our existence do we encounter substantial separateness. At the most obvious 'bodily' level there is no absolute or ontological gap between the 'I' and the 'We' nor is that so at the mental level. At first it seems obvious that my thoughts and feelings are *essentially* mine: that I give rise to them in some *original* sense, *ab initio*. After all no one else suffers my pain and 'knows' what I am thinking. But phenomenological reflection reveals the truth to be otherwise. The 'ego' far from being the source of 'my' stream of consciousness, is in fact an 'object' of consciousness. We can observe that the 'I' is surreptitiously present with all my states of consciousness. This proves that the 'I-ness' can only be represented as the mode of existence of the states of consciousness — the 'mode' has no existence separate from the object whose mode it is. We can agree then that the individual self, the 'I', is no more than an aspect or an act of consciousness, under which the act in question is considered 'owned'.

When we look at the individual self in terms of its *contents* the message is even clearer. First, in self-awareness we are not aware of ourselves as sort of *things* or entities, simply and uniquely *ourselves*. Rather we are aware of the psychological operations of the 'empirical self' filled with a whole host of mental items supposed to be specific to the individual. In general terms, we are aware of ourselves as a consciousness, a 'desire to be', directed upon goals of *personal* achievements (wealth or some other form of power: material or immaterial). But where do the contents of the self come from? When we consider the self in terms of its contents — its plans and motives, goals, ambitions and aspirations, fears and anxieties, in short, its 'attachments' — it becomes clear that the 'self' is a cultural product, a psychological construct. At every stage of its life, it draws from the epistemic and axiological resources of the culture to which the individual belongs. During its constitution, the self is *conditioned* in its attachments.

If this is a correct picture of the empirical self — the self who is the actual chooser, the actual antecedent to action — what are we to say of its 'individuality'? The term 'individuality' receives both a quantitative and a qualitative resolution. In respect of the former, we have found that we have no reason to assert the being of a separate individual, an immaterial substantial 'I'. Does it not, then, weaken the claim of one's passions for personal fulfilment in the wake of egoistic consumerism? Does it not destroy the validity of the ideology which puts the 'me' always over and above the 'we'? And does it not also destroy the belief in the 'quantitative' individuality altogether? I think it will be agreed that our response to these apprehensions must be in the positive.

In the 'qualitative' sense 'individuality' is an evaluative term. It involves norms and standards for our choices, our activities, which refer to human freedom — a spiritual quality of the personal-psychological background from which one's choices flow. Now, without going into the positive character of this 'freedom', we can see this much that a person who acts from the inner compulsions of his conditioned self cannot be said to manifest *individuality*. A person who is chained to his attachments would lack spontaneity of consciousness, would lack the background of freedom. The conditioned self cannot act creatively. His actions are better characterised as 'reactions'. We can then safely conclude that the popular ideas about 'individual', 'individuality' and the consequent 'individualism' are mistaken. And that in turn invites a reassessment of the relationship of the individual with *parampara*. But first some notes on the notion of *parampara*.

The Character of *Parampara*

The advent of modernity in the academic world struck a strong blow to the traditional. Modernity recommended total banishment of the intellectual past (as enshrined in the Cartesian Methodic Doubt). Everything — all social arrangements, intellectual and scientific enterprises — had to be begun from the beginning. Appeal to Reason was the law, so much so that by the beginning of this century 'tradition' and 'traditional' had clearly acquired strong pejorative connotations. But in recent times there seems to be some reaction to this anti-tradition attitude; one often hears the call for a return to the glories of the traditional past, especially in this country. I believe, however, that both the 'rejection' and the 'reaction' are based on inadequate understanding of *parampara*.

In its most popular (and unenlightened) understanding a tradition is taken to involve practices which are merely repetitive and reproductive or some 'object' (artistic or utilitarian) cherished by the community. Now naturally any reproductive process requires a specific *mode* of production which in turn requires certain skills and virtues in the agent — the individual who 'knows' and practices the art of reproduction. The skills and the virtues refer to the qualities of the individual which are required for the success of his activity. If the object in question continues to be desired over a considerable period of time, the entire practice comes to earn the title 'traditional'. But it does not yet explain the title 'tradition'.

The realisation of the object desired is not the whole explanation of the existence of a tradition. It is generally the case that there lies a goal or purpose to be fulfilled beyond the immediate object desired. This goal or purpose is the culminating *telos* or the tradition. And it is the integrating power of the *telos*-consciousness that renders, what are otherwise diverse, practices/activities with a meaning such that they are seen to belong to one identifiable tradition.

In this teleological perspective *parampara* signifies an *ordered* 'stream of consciousness' in which generations of experience and knowledge acquired in the pursuit of some human perfection get organised. This stream of consciousness is directed towards the perfection — the *telos* — for whose fulfilment it exists and receives its identity. In traditional knowledge, skills and meanings are enjoined in a goal-directed purposive manner, which otherwise float randomly in the collective unconscious. In a tradition the accumulated 'wisdom' of a community plays a dynamic role by providing an advanced starting point for the younger generation, as well as, by virtue of its past successes, providing the necessary impetus and inspiration to move towards the *telos*. Thus, a tradition is a dynamic, intelligent human phenomenon. One's participation in a tradition is not, and ought not to be, a ritualistic, monotonously repetitive activity. Instead, in a healthy tradition successive generations move steadily and creatively towards the *telos*. A healthy tradition sustains its life in being constantly enriched by new and better ways of realising its *telos*. The more universal its *telos*, the greater the variety in the modes of its realisation. The complex nature of a tradition and the diversity in its practices need not necessarily be problematical, since the role of a universally meaningful and naturally suggested telos is precisely to serve both as *ratio* and the *ordination* of the contents of the tradition.

Traditions can surely degenerate and turn counterproductive. Historically, in face of dangers of survival, smaller units of a community have tended to withdraw themselves from participation in the larger traditions of the society they belong to. Such isolation, social and psychological, produces 'closed' societies, in which the constituent practices of a tradition lose their teleological insights and become simply tokens of community identity. As the emphasis on the easy availability of the traditional object of desire continues, the individual producer begins to work unimaginatively, i.e., carrying on producing the *same thing* in the *same way* with the *same skills* and virtues. In this sort of situation the *art* of the practices turns into mechanical routine activity signalling the degeneration of the larger tradition. When this happens we lose sight of the value and the relevance of the particular *mode* of production; it no longer engages the creative consciousness of the producer. The 'artist' no longer feels responsible to improve his skills and personal discipline since he does not see his activity as a creative performance constituted within a broader framework of a tradition.

To take an example let us think of the decay of the traditional joint family under the pressure of modern individualism. Central to the joint family is the practice of sharing the total resources of the family with the members of the family. But the meaning of this practice is not explained simply by the contingent fact that several biologically related individuals happen to be living together; nor is it exhausted by its economic persuasions. Clearly, *sharing* refers to the higher purposes of *caring* for the loved ones, which in turn refers to the moral and spiritual dimensions of human life — of order and compassion, of love and justice – pointing to a universal *telos* which is enshrined in the ideal of our ancient dictum: The World is One Family.

To take another example, consider the practice of painting pictures, within an artistic tradition. It is true that painting pictures is often profitable. It may also be the case that it serves some social purpose of the personal-psychological need of self-expression. But none of these provide a satisfactory explanation of why the practice should be construed within an artistic tradition; why it should continue to be valued when none of these services are rendered by it. Why did the caveman paint, for example? It is believed that the construction of the Kailash Mandir in the Ellora caves, carved out of a solid stone hill, took nearly 200 years of sustained effort. Surely such exercises in art cannot be understood without reference to a 'tradition' in a teleological conception.

There is no reason then to treat tradition with contempt, or be pessimistic about it. With a proper understanding of the role of tradition in human life we can see that a tradition has to be innovative or else it would degenerate. In a teleological perspective we can unearth a world of treasures in a tradition and make that our starting point for the innovative strides into the future. We have to realise that for a meaningful 'revolution' we need the background of 'tradition'. A successful revolution is always *within* a tradition and not against it. In a revolution the tradition surpasses the 'givens' of its practices and prepares the ground for a fresh movement with greater intensity and understanding towards its *telos*. In this process it improves upon the very vision of its *telos*.

We can now see that a mindless dedication to the tradition and an emotional rejection of the tradition are both examples of egoistic self-assertion, and not of the 'qualitative' individuality. A real individuality invites a creative engagement with the tradition. In a creative individual choices are made freely and projects are undertaken in the light of full understanding of the meaning of the *telos*. The real individual is not participating in a tradition mechanically with an eye on its utilitarian value alone. Nor is he running away from it. He is not simply reacting from his conditioned background either in conformity or in rejection of the tradition.

The individual's participation in tradition is not an 'optional'. As we have said, the individual self is a culture product; his goals and purposes in life derive from the culture he inhabits. As such he is already rooted in traditions – healthy or degenerate; without tradition it would be only by an extraordinary genius or a lucky fluke that he would manage to realise at all, the goods of human life. Taking the teleological perspective the individual must pursue the tradition creatively. Indeed to be able to retrieve our true individuality from the conditioned background of the cultural self we must derive our meanings and be guided by the overriding *telos* or traditions. In this process, while the wealth of the tradition enriches the individual, his creative pursuit of the *telos* enriches the life of the tradition. Thus, it turns out that the individual and the tradition, far from being incompatible, are in fact necessary to each other. The individual whose behaviour is directed simply by the inner compulsions of the cultural self has no real individuality. The real individuality is freedom, *from* the conditioned self, not *for* the self.

The Indian Spiritual Tradition

What I have said about the retrieval of true individuality, in freedom and creativity, takes us to the heart of the spiritual tradition. It urges the individual to seek retrieval of his humanity from the 'culture of the crowd' of contemporary modernity — the culture of egoism, consumerism, of manipulative human relationships or scandalous scientific humanism, or soulless politics and the cult of irrationalism.

The Indian spiritual tradition is a tradition of *quest* — the quest of the ultimate meaning of life as Truth, Goodness and Beauty. The 'holy trinity' of Truth, Goddness and Beauty is identified as the *telos* of the tradition. The spiritual tradition in itself is 'secular'. It should not be identified with any of the various religious traditions of India. Rather, both the theistic and non-theistic religions of Indian origin, and the meditative systems are the many practical modes of participation in the larger spiritual tradition. In a religion, the spiritual *telos* is given a concrete determination and then a specific mode of operation, a method, is recommended to 'search' for the determinate end.

But a 'quest' must be distinguished from a 'search'. A quest is always a creative enterprise. It is, unlike a search, directed towards a *telos*, the ultimate good of an activity or a set of activities (in this case, of human life as a whole), where the 'good' in question is not given content, a positive definition or concrete meaning. Nor are the 'mode of operation' and the skills and virtues necessary to the quest laid down once and for ever. In a quest one begins with the knowledge made available by the tradition but keeps his mind and heart open to all the revelations and the spontaneous gifts of a holistic movement. One brings one's whole being to bear upon the quest, when 'knowing' and 'self-knowing' move together, when art is devotion, when every action is an element in the *sadhana*. The culture of the quest becomes a massive structure of interlocking traditions of fine, intensely dynamic meanings. The quest, though performed within the parameters of the traditions, is extremely individual-sensitive. It is not in itself a collective exercise. A questful life has no centre, no beginning and no end. One has to allow the creative intelligence — the intelligence that is not merely a function of a network of thought — to take hold of the mind and guide its movements towards the goal.

In a 'search' the situation is somewhat different. One may, for example, search for oil in the Indian Ocean with equipment whose modes of operation are fixed, and one may recognise what one is looking for when one finds it. But in the quest of the ultimate meaning of life one has to launch oneself in the unchartered ocean of existence and through creative management of the knowledge available from the tradition, one moves steadily through the unknown. There is no guarantee of the results — there is always risk in *being*. The quest is sustained and advanced by its own internal logic — its internal arguments, conflicts and insights. Its teleological character, its goal-sensitiveness, supplies it the norms necessary for self-criticism.

Next, the tradition of the quest is not a merely intellectual exercise — it is an experiential tradition. It calls for a *lived* consciousness of Being in all the three aspects of its manifestation. It calls for the individual to be an embodiment of Truth, Goodness and Beauty. An implication of this emphasis on individual experience is that there is no fixed centre of 'authority' in the tradition, in matters of truth and conduct. Each one is to follow his own intuitions, and the role of the teacher is to help the seeker to arrive at his own understanding. The teacher does not concretise the truth and lay down the laws or conduct. So there is always room for moving at a fresh understanding (or a misunderstanding) of the meaning and the contents of the quest — an essential part of growing up in a tradition.

Another important feature of the quest lies in its moral import. This is clear enough when we consider the fact that the quest is carried out *in relationship with others*, not in isolation or a social vacuum. Life is relationship and the quest is an actual life lived in relationship. The internal discipline of the quest, therefore, requires us to relate to others with 'right' intentions, insights and attitudes. What sort of mental states do they signify? In the light of our distinction between 'search' and 'quest', and the self-conscious and self-correcting nature of the spiritual tradition, we can see that the individual must handle his relationships with utmost care: with total responsibility and respect for persons. He must not be manipulative for in the quest of truth of life he is not out for his ego-satisfaction or for some personal gain or pleasure. He must not allow himself to be a victim of emotional turmoil; he must be calm and therefore compassionate. He must manage his attachments even-mindedly, and must not allow the selfish ego to dictate its terms of relationship. And finally no one can remain unimpressed by the universality and comprehensiveness of the quest.

First, reference to Truth, Goodness and Beauty should not be read as reference to three different entities. As it has been generally understood in the tradition, these signify the three primordial aspects of one and the same all-inclusive reality. The spiritual *telos*, therefore, represents an antic unity which can be approached by the human sensitivity under the three exhaustive categories of apprehension: the epistemic, the ethical and the aesthetic respectively.

Next the spiritual *telos* was naturally suggested to the inquiring sages who took cognizance of human life *considered as a whole*, and sought its ultimate meaning. It is interesting to note here that, unlike the Greeks, they did not arrive at the *telos* from a consideration of human *nature* as such, but from the consideration of the primordial *human situation*. By 'human situation' we mean that *original* and essential relationship in which individual self-conscious beings find themselves *vis-a-vis* the undetermined reality, the 'unknown', independently of any metaphysics of how and what they essentially are. And as it is generally understood, human beings find themselves as essentially nothing — a no-thing — and therefore free to choose what they will be, or, to say the least, 'incomplete', standing in a threatening relationship with the vast 'unknown'; they find themselves without any certainties but with enormous 'responsibility' of living a life meaningfully — of making ourselves fit to receive the eternal in the temporal. The sages saw that life was not a 'given' determinate something. It is being constantly realised, shaped and advanced by human activity which is meaningful and purposive. But human consciousness is perpetually disturbed and haunted by the fear of (*samsara*) the world and the insecurity of incompleteness. The individual, as we have seen, is without a unique self-identity. Because of the fear of non-being, he must constantly strive for a permanent identity, though always caught only in a flux of constant 'becoming'. The human being longs for completeness, for some indefinable totality. He needs to be led from darkness into light, from falsehood into truth, from fear into joy.

The sages characterising the human situation in this way naturally arrived at the spiritual *telos* of life. Perceiving the human capacity for advancement and wisdom, they naturally recommend that one need not die in ignorance (especially of his own self), one need not die in an evil and ugly way. Man must live questfully — realising in his own way and in his own measures, Truth, Goodness and Beauty in his life. It may be that very few will ever make it all the way, but they saw very clearly that there is no other way to live, if one wants to live rightly. And setting oneself on the path of a questful life was in itself a blessing, a freedom from fear.

We can now see how the insight of the sages sets up the spiritual tradition of the quest and opens up the landscape of infinite possibilities of life for the individual. Since life is ever new, in constantly changing environment, it was foreseen that human activity will always turn out innumerable 'forms' or engagements with the tradition. The sages were equally aware of the fact that Truth cannot be organised under an 'authority', thus giving the spiritual tradition the shape of an open-ended quest, and equally perceptively, they did not undermine the vulnerability of man — his 'fall' in the pursuit of pleasures. In total understanding of life, therefore, they placed the individual squarely within the fold of the spiritual tradition. There is no salvation in the 'collective', nor does it lie in the greedy egoistic individualism.

10

Longing and Belonging: The Question of Tradition

Alok Rai

THERE is a Faulkner story in which a character gives reasons for why he cannot even think of selling some ancestral land that has been handed down to him. (I quote from memory) He explains that the land is not his to sell, that in a fundamental sense, the land does not belong to him, he belongs to the land. I would like to explore some of this ambiguity of 'belonging' — belong, belonging, belongings — in the context of 'tradition'.

Obviously, there is no general question of 'tradition'. Thus, I am certain that the question of tradition — were it *thinkable* at all, would arise in very different forms in traditional societies. Thus, tradition-bound people, people who belong to a tradition could and probably would argue about matters of detail, about nuances of interpretation — but the question of their particular and even elective relationship to tradition would simply not arise. It is in exactly such a sense that T.S. Eliot remarks that we become conscious of tradition in the moment of its passing — just as we become conscious of the leaves of a tree when it begins to shed them. My exploration of 'belonging' in the context of tradition is addressed mainly to modern people like ourselves who, if they still belong to a tradition, as well they may, must do so in relatively unconscious ways. But it is crucial to my argument to insist on the distinction between such belonging and their conscious longing to belong — the two cannot be identical.

My primary datum for this paper is the etymological connection between 'longing' and 'belonging' — but what is the point of this kind of etymological investigation? After all, as we modern people like to say, what is the significance of such roots? Trees have roots, human beings have legs, it is their histories which define them, not their origins. Ask not where I'm coming from, ask where I'm going to. And yet, roots are stubborn things, and the evolving histories themselves carry some trace of their beginnings, their original impulses. If it didn't sound unacceptably modish, I would have said that I am moved by a kind of archaeological impulse — a faith that if we dig deep enough under and around words, we can discover buried but significant resonances, meanings which, even when they are lost to consciousness, are nevertheless active. At the very least, they can help to illuminate some of the ambiguities — and hidden agendas — of contemporary usage. Again, I derive strength from the Heideggerean enterprise, as represented by Rorty, that our words carry submerged meanings which are nevertheless operative, albeit in deep and obscure ways. Rorty writes:

> Ever since philosophy won its quarrel with poetry, it has been the thought that counts . . . words are mere vehicles for something less fragile and transitory. . . .
>
> Rorty quotes Heidegger on the proper business of philosophy:" to preserve the force of the most elemental words . . . and to keep the common understanding from levelling them off. . . .

When a word is used frequently and easily, Rorty explains, when it becomes a familiar, ready-to-hand instrument for achieving our purpose, we can no longer hear it...

The implication, quite clearly, is that common, everyday, `ordinary language' is an archive of thought, of the ways in which the relations between ourselves and our worlds have been conceived. As will be apparent, I have sought to create these philosophical outworks — big names, big guns — in order to legitimise my modest endeavour to recover the 'force' of 'belonging'.

'Belonging' — both the word and the emotion — is only too familiar, even if the emotion is known mainly through an absence. Thus, nostalgia is a familiar trope in modern writing: the obscure sense of homelessness, the familiar yearning to return to some lost home, some condition of innocent plenitude and amplitude. Thus, the anguish of the exile is rather older than its current post-modern celebration:

> Wanderers outside the gates,
> In hollow landscapes without memory,
> We carry each of us an urn

Of native soil anciently gathered.
Not wide enough to build a dwelling on . . .
But cool and soft, in which we hear
Murmurs of home, like oceans in a shell

It comes as something of a shock to realise that this sense of 'belonging' — of appertaining, of relationship, especially membership and acceptance by a group or society — is relatively modern. (The OED dates it to 1879). But the first use recorded there, in the precise sense we are seeking to understand — 'belongingness' — comes from 1958: 'What a child needs is a settled home, a feeling of permanence, security, of belonging'. . . .

Dr Johnson records six senses of the verb 'to belong':

1. to be the property of;
2. to be the province or business of — thus, this belongs elsewhere;
3. to adhere, or be appendent to;
4. to have relation to;
5. to be the quality or attributes of; and
6. to be referred

In a general sort of way, 'belong' is equivalent to 'goes along with'.

In trying to think of some purpose about the modern sense of the word 'belonging', and the modern experience of unbelonging, it is interesting to look a little closely at the formation of the word 'belong'. ('Unbelonging', though the emotion is common enough, has not yet been canonised by inclusion in the OED. Unbelonging doesn't belong.) 'Belong' is related to 'long', and one of the early and now obsolete senses of belong is 'equally long, corresponding in length'. In MHG, the verb 'to long' is present in the sense of 'reach, extend, suffice' - and the familiar modern verb 'to long' in the sense of having a desire for, to yearn for, is related by Skeat and others, to reach out with one's mind, etc. Finally, the OED records obsolete usages in which 'long' itself seems to be like 'belong' in several senses.

Belong is formed by adding the prefix 'be-' to 'long'. 'Be-' is a puzzling sort of prefix, not least because it is still a living element, still capable of generating new meanings. This is the OED on the prefix 'be-': The original meaning of 'be' is about, but it is frequently weakened, in prepositions and adverbs, into a general expression of position, at or near — as in before, behind, below, between, beyond. In verbs, various senses of 'about' are often retained - as in beset, be-stir. In bedaub, bespatter, the notion of 'all about, all round' or 'throughout' naturally intensifies the sense of the verb - and so 'be-' becomes more or less a simple intensive, as in bemuddle. In certain other words, the force of 'be-' passes over to an object, and renders an intransitive verb transitive, as in bespeak, belie, bemoan. Hence, it is used to form transitive verbs on adjectives and substantives, as in dim-bedim, fool-befool, etc. Of these, a special section consists of verbs having a privative force — as in behead.

Clearly then, if we keep the adjectival and verbal senses of 'long' in mind - having extension, and desiring — and the relevant different senses of the prefix 'be-', the resultant 'belong' becomes something of a semantic puzzle. To put it schematically:

long (adj) + be- (i.e., rendered transitive) = make long;

Long (vb) is an instransitive verb which the prefix "be-" should render transitive, but as things stand, this transitivity is invisible and unavailable, and the relations between the two intransitive verbs — long and belong — are odd and paradoxical. Thus, if *X* gives me a feeling of belonging, then one may, in a strict etymological sense, say that *X* 'belongs' me. This is obviously completely different from saying that *X* 'belongs to' me. Indeed, in the sense of the Faulkner story that I started out with, it might be more accurate to say that 'I belong to *X*'.

'Longing', as desire, has something to do with a carving for 'belongings'. But the having of such belongings leads, at least momentarily, to the cessation of desire, of longing. Thus, in this sense, there is a contradictory relation between longing and belonging. Belonging appears to be, in a common sense sort of way, the end (both meanings: goal, cessation) of longing: a satisfied longing is a superfluous longing, a superannuated longing. However, if we see a desire for extension, for inclusion in something larger than oneself as one of the operative senses of belonging, then the satisfaction of 'longing' (desire) in belonging, only enables this process of 'extension' to get under way. Read in this way, belonging is not the end of longing, it is only the beginning.

(As will be evident, I am rather more interested in the semantic trace of desire and extension in belonging — but wish to note, *en passant*, the apparent relation between the widespread hunger for belonging, as evident in the runaway proliferation of the politics of identity, and the functioning of the economic regimes which have been unable to provide adequate belongings. Thus, one may hazard the proposition that there appears to be a connection between the need for belonging and the having of excessive or insufficient material belongings.

However, to return to the trace of desire and extension in belong — is belong a transitive or an intransitive verb? As noted earlier, the prefix 'be-' should render 'long (vb, desire') transitive, but if one seeks to know what could be the *object* of such a transitivised 'belonging', the answer can only be belonging itself: the activity of belonging — thus recovered — seeks the condition of belonging. What is gained by such a procedure is, I suggest, a recovery of the diachronic, active nature of the quest for the condition of belonging. In such a construction, belonging is a dynamic state, a reaching out, rather than a passive and complacent state of rest. The extension sense of long — and the consequent possible sense of 'be-long' — make long, or larger than oneself — is relevant here. So that what becomes thinkable is not only a restless longing, a reaching-out for belonging, but also this belongingness itself is understood, on good etymological grounds, as the need or desire to become part of something larger than oneself.

What, finally, shall we make of this lost transitivity, this passivisation of 'belong' and 'belonging', this operation whereby' the verb-origins of 'belonging' get elided and the process reifies into a substantive, almost a thing, at best a state or condition? Or what, to put it another way, is gained by recovering this lost transitivity, a sense of process and activity? In the word as it is available to our common sense today, we can still recognise the hunger, the longing — but it is a struggle to recover an awareness of the social and historical processes that create this hunger for belonging — and indeed, bear crucially upon the ways in which that hunger can seek satisfaction in today's world.

(Thus, it is significant that 'identity' has gone from signalling sameness to becoming a sign of the politics of destructive difference.)

I must, at last, seek to answer the question I raised at the outset — what is the point of such an etymological investigation? What *argument* can I derive from a thus laboriously established trace of desire and extension in the familiar word 'belonging'? As far as I'm concerned, this is at least a pleasant coincidence; it might even be a serendipitous confirmation, a clue embedded in the sedimented layers of one language of a connection which I would press on other grounds as well. Thus, in seeking to understand the politics of identity, of cultural belonging, in our time, we must perforce notice the renewed concern with the question of tradition: the traditions dusted and aired, refurbished, trimmed-down, tricked-out, invented, fabricated. (My reference, I must state unambiguously, is to the wider world beyond the confines of the present seminar). But the etymology I have offered enables us to notice something more: a connection between the apparatuses responsible for the exacerbation of desire — and, inevitably, of its concomitant frustration — and the precise forms in which collective identities are both made available — through complex sociological processes, through life-worlds and communities smashed and reconfigured — as well as the ways in which such collective identities are, in ways benign and all too frequently malign, sought.

11

Tradition, Modernity and the Individual: An Indian Viewpoint

Ashok R. Kelkar

Demystifying Tradition

TRADITION is so much a part of human life that in order to understand what tradition is all about one simply has to understand what human life is like.

A human being is a living being like any other kind of living being, and human life is thus part and parcel of life on earth. (This is something that artists, naturalists, and mothers never lose sight of.) As a living being, a human being is in constant interaction with the rest of the world — especially the rest of the world to which living beings have access, that is to say, the environment of that human being. Living just consists in this interaction, which maintains a certain harmony between the living being and its environment. This interaction is no mere exchange of matter, energy, and information. ('Information' here stands for a certain patterning or sharable arrangement — as with shadows cast or footprints left by an animal or with shapes or sounds picked up by its retina or cochlea). Rather, this interaction is action and reaction in either direction. Whenever and wherever the interaction diminishes or ceases, life diminishes or ceases. If life ceases, this island of some orderly arrangement within an ocean of comparative disorder merges with that ocean. Absence of that harmony spells danger or even failure for the living being, even for the kind it belongs to or for the population it belongs to. ('Population' here stands for all the plants and animals inhabiting a given locality in a given period in symbiotic or competing or conflicting arrangement.)

The interaction consists of the following:

1. The living being responds to the environment: it overtly manipulates in action and covertly monitors the environment in reaction.
2. The environment affects the living being in action and reaction: it offers overt opportunity or resistance or covert sustenance or adversity.

Harmonious interaction spells welfare and success. Short of major catastrophes, life goes on in an even tenor: living beings adjust and the environment supports. The earth proves to be a home. The environment typically includes other living beings, typically the ones belonging to the same kind or to the same population. The other living beings have a special status for the interacting living being.

But then a human being is a living being unlike any other kind of living being. (This is something that preachers, humanists, and dreamers never tire of reminding us of.) To begin with, humans are mammals and so are 'higher' animals with sexual reproduction and physical intimacy with dependent sucklings. Overt manipulation in response amounts here to behaviour (*cheshtita*) and covert monitoring in response to experience (*anubhava*). Underlying their behaviour and experience are certain inner compulsions, namely, drives or abilities along with their modification through learning. The external compulsions from the environment are often modified by living beings through selection (as of a locality with water supply) and reshaping (as a beaver's dam). What is more, humans are no ordinary mammals. They aspire to thrive in all sorts of environment: what is more, like rats or sparrows or cockroaches, they appear to have done so in spite of being weaklings when nature puts on a cruel face, their hereditary equipment falling far too short. Just how do human beings manage this feat? They are islands of more intricate and so more delicate order, which is both a compensation and a liability.

The young one of a human develops the capacities for bearing/begetting, for mating, and for parenting in that order and at intervals which is awkward. A human is born unfinished, so to say: there are few detailed innate programmes (comparable to nest-building), rather more of broad directions, that need to be activated and shaped by appropriate environmental conditions (consider how clumsy human parenting can be). The mating urge is round the year; the procreativity depends not on the solar cycle but the lunar cycle. The day of this daytime mammal is not exhausted in feeding, resting, saving of the skin, and mating (*ahara-nidra-bhaya-maithunam-ca*) with time enough on hand to explore the outer and inner worlds. There is an inner world: consciousness monitors not only the here and now but also the there and then, even contemplates what is nowhere and may never be. Visual imaging and outer/inner speech assist. There is a covert outer world: play enters into mating and makes for play-acting and make believe, for example. Behaviour often turns into result-oriented coping activity (*karman*) and experience often turns into problem-oriented thought. Harmonious interaction between humans and their environment is promoted not only through short-term adjustment to and support from the environment but also through long-term restructuring of the environment (consumer goods and producer goods) and of humankind. The restructuring of humans consists in the forming of personalities, societies, and cultures. The inner compulsions (drives and abilities) are turned by learning conditions into inclinations and capacities and these add up to a personality. Dependence of the young leads to adult intimacy and to interdependence. The concurrent socialisation and individualisation of the child and the adult precipitates into a society. Coping with life and cognising of the world interact into a certain nurturing and conditioning of personality and of society. That constitutes a culture.

Given the intricacy and consequent delicacy of the fabric of human life, humans end up making and conceding claims that are often quite contrary to each other and this makes life even more intricate! (No wonder that Kant threw up his hands in horror at the crooked timber that humanity is made of.) We are concerned here with two of these antinomies, because they allow tradition to step in, take over, and give succour to these weaklings, 'higher' weaklings to be sure. These two are the antinomy of history and the antinomy of self-identity. Let it be clear that the hallmark of an antinomy is that neither of the paired truths has much meaning without the other.

The antinomy of history helps human beings to deal with the arrow of time — which ensures that not all the king's men can put humpty-dumpty together again. ('Dealing with' covers both manipulating and monitoring, coping with and cognising.) The paired truths can be stated quite simply as follows:

(i) There is no wiping the slate: man's present becomes past and stays with him as memory and as the situation at hand. At the sametime —.

(ii) There is no turning back: man's future becomes present and wipes the slate clean of what were earlier certain possibilities or near-certainties.

The first perception yields the sense of an uninterrupted series of continuity: the same old set-up leaves you comforted or despairing by turns. The second perception yields the sense of constant shift or open-endedness: the possibility of novelty leaves you hopeful or uncomfortable by turns. In short, man has a sense of abiding inheritance and unending change whether as a person or as a member of society. All ages qualify as ages of transition, whether in biography or in history. Human beings have a story to live and a story to tell.

The antinomy of self-identity helps human beings to deal with the thorn of self-consciousness — which is consciousness turning on itself. The paired truths of this antinomy are as follows:

(i) There is pride in the desire to find oneself, to preserve, accentuate, even celebrate our separation and our distinction from others: the smallest of us is important ('always as an end, never merely as a means', says Kant; may whoever whatever deeply wants get it', says Jnaneshvara). At the same time —

(ii) There is modesty in the desire to lose oneself, to merge oneself in the life of the company one keeps and to recognise one's resemblance to others: the greatest of us is unimportant ('O! why was I born with a different face? / Why was I not born like the rest of the race?', says Blake in some anguish).

The first perception yields the sense of every man being an island: man's ability to recognise faces and inability to have access to another's consciousness reinforces this perception. Man has a tragic sense of proud isolation or a mystical bliss of *kaivalya*. The second perception yields the sense of no man being an island: man's ability to recognise resemblances, shallow or deep, with oneself and drive to seek out the company of those that resemble oneself. Man has a comic sense of unassuming conviviality or a mystical bliss of *nirvana*.

The two antinomies together elicit from human beings the hide-and-seek of tradition and modernity. Today's tradition was modernity the day before yesterday, and today's modernity will be tradition the day after tomorrow. Tradition and modernity are relative to each other: they constitute an opposition and not a true antinomy.

The word *traditio* in Latin means 'giving across', that is, handing over, delivering, or even betraying (the word *treason* being a derivative). By emphasising continuity, tradition supports a person and helps him to lose himself, and in so doing it could betray him or prevent him from finding himself by making a break with the past. Tradition tends to be opposed to innovation or experiment and often lapses into letting things take their course.

The word *parampara* in Sanskrit means, one following the other from ear to ear, from hand to hand, from teacher to disciple and so forth. The Indian tradition is like a palimpsest and has unresolved tensions built into itself. Depending on the context, *parampara* is opposed to *shastra* (conscious discipline), *deshya* (regional or local), or *adhunika/navya* (recent/new). The word *smirti/smarana* is sometimes a close synonym, given its primary meaning of 'remembering or recalling'.

The Arabic words *silsilah* (chain, series), *rashm* (marked out manner), or *tariqah* (manner) and the Persian word *dastur* (rule handed down) have varying underlying metaphors for conveying the notion of tradition.

Remystifying Tradition

But then one often uses the pairing of tradition and modernity not in the original relative sense in which they play hide-and-seek but in an imposed absolute sense. One distinguishes between traditional societies (of Ancient or Medieval India or Europe and their present-day survivals, for example) and modern societies (of Modern Europe or India and their forerunners, for example). In so doing one agrees to overlook certain palpable or even deep-seated differences between India and Europe (even in comparable phases, for example), or to overlook the chronological mismatch (modern India emerging much later than modern Europe, for example). In recognising survivals from traditional society there is at least historical continuity to fall back upon as with the ceremonial of British royalty or with the endogamy and group loyalty in the Hindu caste system. But how does one recognise anticipations of modernity or throwbacks to tradition? Indeed if 'recognise' is the right word; perhaps 'ascribe' is the word to use in attributing modern sentiments to Saint Francis of Assisi or Kabir or interpreting as premature modernising the transition from the Athens of Pericles to the Athens of Alcibiades (which so disturbed the conservative Socrates) or the impact on the Brahmanical society of the culture of the *shramana* (which led to a Brahmanical counter-reformation). Likewise, when one recognises throwbacks in attributing traditional sentiments to Charles de Gaulle or interpreting Marxism as a latter-day religion with affinities to Judaism and Christianity. In all such ascribing or, again, in recognising a certain homogeneity between pre-modern Europe and India or between modern Europe and India, one chooses to focus on large abstractions. One is not thinking of tradition and modernity in a relative sense so much as of Tradition and Modernity (with capital T or M) in an absolute sense.

How does one understand these two abstractions then? Any historically attested feature or cluster of features of personality, society, or culture are seen as indices of whole ways of coping with life and whole ways of cognising the world. What is more, one is recognising a major worldwide shift, a watershed so to say, give or take a couple of centuries, in the course of the major world civilisations of history such as the European or the Indian. In thinking of Tradition and Modernity in this absolute sense as a fact of the history of humankind, one is thinking of two whole lifestyles and correspondingly two whole world-views. Spelling out a lifestyle or a world-view is of course a philosophical activity. Now it will have been noticed that we have steadily moved from manipulating/ monitoring through behaviour/experience and activity/thought and coping with life/cognising of the world finally on to lifestyle/ world-view. Earlier we have seen that any coping with life affects and conditions cognising of the world and that any cognising of the world affects and conditions coping with life. It is this interaction between coping and cognising that leads to the emergence of lifestyles and world-views, that is to say, the formation of whole schemata out of what Levi-Strauss calls the *bricolage* of stray rules of thumb. (Beginning with stray, simple rules like 'Feed a cold and starve a fever' or 'Bleeding is profuse when it is full moon or new moon', one ends up with whole philosophies of health and healing.)

In what follows, we spell out the schemata of Tradition and Modernity. We shall begin with the world-views and move on to lifestyles and under each lifestyle we shall take up personality and society before we end up with culture and material culture. (By 'material culture' we mean the restructuring of the environment.) We hope that this order of presentation will justify itself: while all of these undoubtedly condition each other, the later-mentioned tend to depend more on the earlier-mentioned than the other way round.

World-view: Tradition: Non-sensory perception of some reality behind appearances is the foundation of valid cognising (*episteme, Prama*). Man as we see him is but a train of apparent behaviour and the world around man is but a scattered outlay of appearances. Appearances are best cognised and gaps in apparent casual chains (action at a distance or after an interval or both) filled when the reality is seen as the manifestation of pervasive energy (*energeia, potestas, shakti*) latent in the unmanifest (say, a seed/a young man) as potency or tendency that gets released by a trigger (say, soil and moisture/a nubile young woman). Changes in human life are best seen as a stationary cycle.

World-view:Modernity: Observation and inference, both appropriately elaborated, are the foundations of valid cognising both of the world and of man in the world. The phenomena grasped through observation and inference are to be cognised by postulating causal regularities and forces (such as gravitation and electricity, strong and weak interaction, the eros and thanatos of Freud's psychology) underlying the world and man in the world. Changes in human life are best seen as an oscillatory progress.

Lifestyle:Tradition: Man, being a living being like no other, needs to come to terms with himself through gaining contact with the pervasive energy that makes life possible. And through arranging his coping with the world he is in to the extent needed (of which asceticism is the minimal strategy). Such is the foundation of gainful coping (*siddhi*). Man's freedom consists in the recognition of necessity, that is, the necessity of liking what he has got.

Lifestyle:Modernity: Man, being a living being like any other, needs to come to terms with the environment through adapting himself to it. And through adapting the environment to himself, necessity being the mother of invention, that is, managing to get what he likes. Such is the foundation of gainful coping (success). Man's freedom consists in the opportunity to exercise his spontaneity, that is in external necessity not standing in the way of internal necessity.

Lifestyle: Personality and Society: Tradition: (i) Let a person be humble, following the imperative 'To thyself be enough'. For a person to be mature is to be socially acceptable, orderly and conforming. For a person to be immature is to be not socialised enough for want of individualisation, and to accept immortality for a person/community with smug or panicky literalism. (ii) Let interpersonal relations be governed by decorum and due distance. In particular, let a person not do unto others what he would not be done unto and try to do unto others what he would be done unto. (Compare the Golden Rule and *atmaupamya*.) For any society to be orderly is to be bound by custom and law, and governed by the kindly ruler assisted by the upright official. Law is, ultimately, community-wide custom. For a society to be devoid of order is to have extremes of regimentation (eliciting obedience or shirking) or disorder (encouraging victim's abjectness or criminal's violence) or blind trust (with the credulous and the impostors). (iii) Human peaks are seen in seers, saints, and heroes; human valleys are simple, conservative, ordinary people. (A mystic could be a peak or belong to the valley.) (iv) Happiness and sorrow are undivided. Let external necessity be passively accepted. One may identify internal necessity with external necessity (*advaita*) or refuse to do so (*dvaita*, Christianity) in one's discourse.

Lifestyle: Personality and Society: Modern: (i) Let a person have an unencumbered self, following the imperative 'To thyself be true'. For a person to be mature is to be socially responsible without ceasing to be free or even subversive. For a person to be immature is to be not individualised enough for want of socialisation, and to accept mortality for a person/community with panicky or smug literalism. (ii) Let interpersonal relations be governed by privacy and due intimacy. In particular, let a person surmise with caution what the other would or would not be done unto; inclinations differ. For any society to be orderly is to be bound by alliance or contract and role and governed by the rule of law and its administration by efficient officialdom. Law is, ultimately, community-wide contract. For a society to be devoid of order is to have extremes of fashion (eliciting conformity or eccentricity) or disorder (encouraging an indifference that permits no-holds-barred competition or smooth criminality) or blind mistrust (from skeptics or cynics). (iii) Human peaks are seen in thinkers, artists and leaders; human valleys are no-nonsense commonsensical ordinary people. (A mystic can choose to be a peak if he likes.) (iv) Freedom and justice are undivided. The good of the many is the happiness of the many (*bahujanahitaya bahujanasukhaya* or 'for the greatest happiness of the greatest numbers' is a problematic formulation). Let internal necessity be actively accepted. One may identify external necessity with internal necessity (optimism) or refuse to do so (pessimism) in one's discourse.

Lifestyle: Culture and Material Culture:Tradition: (i) The orderly and secure society moulds the individual and helps him to enter into bonds of loyalty. Innovation is little more than renovation of tradition. (Sense of on-going history is poorly developed.) (ii) The individual acquires or proposes a *modus vivendi* (*niti*) or a modus operandi (*riti* or *paddhati*) and the community ratifies it. Personal activism and community level 'revival' attempts are recognised modes of change. The local community (such as a guild or a village) offers uniformity and solidarity; the larger community (such as a city or the *imperium*) offers diversity and assurance. (Solidarity stands for the way of 'each for all and all for each'; assurance stands for the way of each assuring compliance and insuring protection.) The urban habitat is seen as a warp in a rural landscape. (iii) A culture enshrines the world-view in myths and the lifestyle in ritual. It codifies its cognising in a doctrine (*orthodoxos, shastra*) along with residual lore (*mathema, vidya*) and its coping in craft (*tekhne, shilpa*) and magic (*abhichara*).

Lifestyle: Culture and Material Culture: Modernity: (i) The orderly and secure society helps the individual to mature properly and to enter into bonds of love. Tradition is no more than an innovation that has come to stay. (Sense of abiding heritage is poorly developed.) (ii) The individual acquires or proposes a *modus vivendi* or a *modus operandi* and the community endorses it. Personal activism and community-level planning are recognised modes of change. The local community (such as a neighbourhood or a profession) offers a diversity to choose from and loose-knit alliances, the larger community (such as a city or the civil society) offers the same diversified menu everywhere and the assurance of free access and anonymity. The rural habitat is seen as gaps yawning within the urban landscape. (iii) A culture enshrines the world-view and the lifestyle in an ideology. It codifies its cognising in science and lore and its coping in technique and craft.

We have come to the end of our spare inventory; there is, however, much more in it than meets the casual eye. The inventory is spare for a good reason: we have resolutely employed high-level abstractions in preserving our philosophical stance. In working towards the highest common factors of European and Indian Tradition and of European and Indian Modernity, we have entertained the hope that the other contemporary world civilisations, the East Asian and the South-West Asian, can be accommodated within this synopsis both in respect of Tradition and of Modernity without resorting to procrustean measures. (The rubrics, Indian, European and so on, of course ignore the geographical fluctuations due to shifts in environment, demography, power distribution, and culture access.) I shall be happy if those more closely familiar with the East Asian and the South-West Asian civilisations find out whether the hope entertained is justified or not.

At the same time, the inventory is richer than appears to be the case. Formulations have been made with care. Notice, for example, the difference between 'man and the world around man' viewed by Tradition and 'the world and the man in the world' viewed by Modernity; again, *niti* as *modus vivendi* is being taken in the broader traditional sense and not in the later sense confining *niti* to morality or *sadharana niti* and the two Latin legal terms are being only slightly stretched. We have used high-level abstract rubrics like world-view, interpersonal, freedom, order — permitting us to give due weightage to certain matters that are ordinarily sidelined such as the identification of human peaks or immaturity in a person or loss of true order in society in Tradition and Modernity. (Note how regimentation and regimented fashion are examples of disorder and not of true social order.)

We have certainly resisted the temptation of taking the easy way out and focus on rubrics like Epistemology, Logic, and Cosmology; Family, State and Economy; Religion, Art, and Technology that are canonical in European Modernity. If we wish to be truly anthropocentric rather than ethnocentric, we need also to resist the lure of 'contemporary relevance' and keep away from the idols of the marketplace or the corridors of power or the roundtable of discussion. Ecology, Feminism, market forces, controlled economy, forms of democracy, globalisation, the fate of popular culture, and the rest are useful low-level abstractions in their place. The inventory embodies our reflections on the large revolution of our times, namely, the worldwide transition from Tradition to Modernity, give or take a couple of centuries. These reflections may illuminate the contemporary issue in a surprising manner. Thus, given the absence of the traditional involvement in the environment as seen in the peasant, modern ecology programmes may turn out to be no more than a plea for enlightened real estate management or weekend tourism for stress-reduction. Rather than foreclosing the contemporary issues, we could try and see how far they could be subsumed under the larger abstractions and the broader reflections.

The Individual at the Crossroads

If we have taken some care to avoid Eurocentricity, then why have we put forward an Indian viewpoint? An Indian viewpoint need not be the Indocentric viewpoint. A present-day Indian can be, as in the present case, someone that enjoys a double heritage, the Indian tradition and the European tradition, in addition to participating in Indian Modernity. Our preoccupation thus far with our shared Humanity (especially as we sought to demystify tradition in the opening portion) and with our shared Tradition and Modernity (especially as we wondered about remystifying them) must not blind us to our problem as individuals.

There is no putting the clock back in socio-cultural action any more than in personal action. There is no going back from Modernity to Tradition against the arrow of time. But then there is no wiping the slate clean in socio-cultural action any more than in personal action. There is no simple jettisoning the baggage of Tradition to make room for Modernity. The arrow of time is also the seal of time. There is an issue all right facing us.

The individual of today, whether thinker, artist, or leader or (as carried over from Tradition) seer, saint, or hero, is at the crossroads. (A person unselfconsciously inhabiting the valley faces an issue, but he has no problem unless he sees himself as rising above the rest ever so little.) Does he turn his back on Tradition and embrace Modernity or try to? Does he turn his back on Modernity and embrace Tradition or try to? Does he try to resolve the opposition? (Recall that Tradition and Modernity is certainly an opposition, but it is not an antinomy.) That is the problem. The least satisfactory resolution is trying an uneasy compromise or a camouflage of Tradition as a version of Modernity or a camouflage of Modernity as a renovation of Tradition. These no doubt present the easy way out, and many inhabitants of the valley appear to unselfconsciously adopt them: they are more keen on losing themselves than on finding themselves.

How about more limited resolutions? An example of such a strictly limited resolution will be a resolution between *Ayurveda*, the doctrine of health and healing in Indian Tradition, together with a whole lore of healing on the one hand and the Science of health and healing in European Modernity together with a whole lore of healing on the other hand. Indeed up to a point there is no problem at all — as when an Ayurvedic physician freely adopts certain diagnostic techniques from European Modernity or when a Modern physician incorporates Ayurvedic herbs into his pharmacopoeia and quietly discards certain magical practices. If one stops to consider how the doctrine of health and healing in European tradition gradually transformed itself into the Modern science, one could see how more limited resolutions could be attempted. Examples from other canonically recognised areas like the meditational or prophylactic practices of Yoga or Music or Business and Management lore could be thought of. (Yoga as a world-view and lifestyle is of course quite another matter.)

How about more ambitious and yet more satisfactory resolutions? Such resolutions, if forthcoming, will be at once more demanding and more rewarding. I have no intention even to attempt such a resolution between Tradition and Modernity; the search will probably be on the agenda for another half-century, but I have certain broad observations to offer. (Is the younger generation listening?)

(1) Man may be a frail reed and Tradition has certainly offered a protective umbrella in certain world civilisations. May be he has outlived its utility and so considered Modernity to be a better umbrella for the present juncture in the history of humankind. Why a better cover? European Modernity, at least from the time of Hegel, has offered an answer: Tradition and Modernity are to be seen as stages in the story of man's quest for freedom and order. (Traditional India may translate this as a quest for *mukti* and *dharma*, *nibbana* and *dhamma*.) There is no sign that the quest is at an end; indeed there are already signs that a search for a better cover is on. (Adapting the *Gita* saying to a novel context, one may say: *vasamsi jirnani yatha vihaya navani grhnani naro' parani*.)

(2) This new cover may not turn out to be a resolution of the opposition between Tradition and Modernity at all, though it could very well be that, considering that this is not an antinomy but an opposition. Personally, I often find myself defending Tradition in a gathering of Modernity-zealots and Modernity in a gathering of Tradition-zealots. What do I do in a mixed gathering? I just proclaim: wake up from your dogmatic slumber, you have nothing to lose but your fear of freedom! (Or fear of order, as the case may be.)

(3) The philosophical tools of European Modernity are not quite satisfactory for resolving or transcending the opposition between Tradition and Modernity. The major obstacles, as I see them, are two: the either-or approach with the endemic pendulum swing (it is to the credit of Kant and Niels Bohr that they spotted the problem) and the matter/mind polarity of ontology and the objective/subjective polarity of epistemology (the problem has been spotted by modern physics and Rusellian epistemology).

The Indian philosophical tool kit has something more promising, think: (a) Indian thinkers have offered two platforms for transcending the either-or approach: the lower platform of the sighted man looking at the whole elephant and taking in a more inclusive view and the higher platform of *anekanta* (a useful parable will be the cartographer's alternate projections for mapping the earth on a flat sheet). (b) They offer a three-way ontology of the mundane (*laukika*), the constructed (*aupacharika*), and the transmundane (*adhyatmika*). (c) And a two-way aetiology of genesis (*utpatti/parinati*) and manifestation (*abhivyakti*) — comparable respectively to the relation of inferability (or functional relationship) and the relation of participation (Plato's *methexis/koinonia* in *Phaedo* and elsewhere in Traditional Europe). These tools offer greater flexibility in handling the complexities of human life. (Modern Europe has discarded the relation of participation.)

(4) We have noted earlier that there are already signs that a search for a better cover than Modernity is on. Since the emergence of Modernity in human history was closely associated with the European civilisation, it was to be expected that the questioning of Modernity first occurred in that civilisation and that the questioning often took the form of a questioning of the European civilisation. A radical questioning of the world-view and lifestyle of Modernity, unaccompanied by any proposal for a return to Tradition, started in nineteenth century Europe — probably with Nietzsche, who proposed a 'transvaluation of values'. The current wave of post-modernisms sounds more like adventurist whistlings in the dark than resolute attempts to work one's way out; they typically encourage such followers as are looking for intellectual chic or quick-fix protection from the fear of order.

In any case, realising that we are at the crossroads is a necessary first step. Even the longest journey begins with a small step.

Colophon

It is obvious that I ought to be giving citation for attested traits from primary sources (for example, for *atmaupamya* and the Golden Rule under Tradition and the questioning of this under Modernity). Then there are the citations for the various insights I owe to the secondary sources though I have not always wholly adhered to these (for example, for the foundations of the social order under Tradition and Modernity my immediate debt is to Auden and indirect debt is to Tonnies and Maine). It is interesting to note how some of the details of the opening account of life and human life drawing upon modern science have been anticipated in the tradition (for example, death as dissolution into cosmic elements or as reduction to dust). Tracking all these down will take a while: I hope to do that later. I crave the reader's indulgence for this lacuna.

12

Patterns and the Pattern

Keshav Malik

THIS paper may amount to aiming shots in the dark, and that despite the guidelines for the seminar. The subject proposed could appear to be shrouded in the mists of abstraction, even as it is magnetic to the emotions. Again, having had no foreknowledge as to who the other participants to the seminar were to be, from which spheres of activity, at home in which particular style or styles of discourse, I have had apprehensions that the discussion may spin in circles, arrested amid cross-purposes, misconceptions, generalities and so on. Such a lot evidently can be stuffed in the expression individual and *parampara*, so charged are they with ambiguity, that all of us could be right without arriving at any clear agreement, not having achieved any richer meaning through our deliberations. The subject, or the occasion, seems to bristle with difficulties.

One of the reasons for this difficulty is the sheer ideality of the topic for discussion. Questions relating to things, enquiry pertaining to fact or plain occurrence are rather more within the rightful purview of the specialised — trained, practised — mind, than those imponderables relating to mankind, and all of which are so to say 'political' in nature, and which last fact in turn means that they are in a religious sphere—that is, in an area involving wish, desire, spiration choice, and so on. The ambiguity of the expression the individual inheres in one broad fact: of his or her being unformed or open-ended in at least the deeper, qualitative essence.

So I ask, are we gathered here to solve neutral problems (of whatever genre) or are we here to reveal to ourselves the contours of our own secret personalities, inner bents, some obdurate unmalleable psychic material which is not amenable to cultural tampering or social improvement, but which instead must be accepted to be the very premise, the departure as well as arrival point of all our laborious efforts, of all our promethean will to being and becoming and so on. Till we grant or discover some such subjective groundwork of self, our forays into the ambiguous will remain brilliant but barren exercises that are only partly relevant to behaviour. Is there any psychic substance in us, the gathered individuals, that eludes our conscious reasoning faculties, one that will give us the slip at the last moment, that comes before all logic and rational planning and which in truth is the patron towards whom we cannot stand in a condescending relationship? If we do establish such an entity (however impalpable, and nevertheless vital, with attributes which it would be hard for us to define or enumerate too neatly) then we can return afresh to continue our struggle with our future prospects. A stable point, however complex and difficult of description or definition it might be, needs to be assumed and affirmed, that is before any such futures can be hypothesised, before any axiology or value frame can be outlined in all its intricate hierarchy of dimension.

How do we arrive at such a slippery customer? What analysis, inference, experimentation, or deduction will aid us in such a quest? Admittedly the query is fruitless in one sense. The thing has to be almost accepted on personal faith and which last I define as that propensity in the reasonable, acculturated adult (who though he accepts most things only on tested facts or if faith, then a faith which is really goodwill towards those expert in one field or another) takes the fact or the value or sacredness of self or the inner substance from his own living; his own, or that recorded in the testaments of literature — those parables, human chronicles or the legends of unusual lives. Now this faith, unlike the faith which offers positive knowledge, is open to error but it is also the harbinger or promoter of value, the word I have been fighting back so far. The question of worth arises with the coming of a consciousness shared in common, and which is well above the 'drives and needs', as scientific disciplines may define them.

What sort of human future do we have in mind, the future of a particular race or the future envisioned through the screen of value as experienced by individuals at moments of grace in their lives; value which could be said to be imbibed by scanning the story of the human sojourn on earth. The shared value that I have in mind, is shared not quantitatively, *en mass* (like the values which simpler goals, drives and needs acquire) but value which distinctly pertains to those functions of the personality, those interchanges — the moral processes — between the head and the heart which lead to the creation or the coming into being (however tentatively) of the inner person. Here then is the prime value, prime because at moments it helps one to be totally immune to one's own socio-economic or bio-existence. The so-called inner person is a functioning, going psychic concern within the continuum or context of something which could not be exchanged for some other good. I believe this concern must be postulated as the value of collective effort.

The somatic drives and urgencies of human existence, and the catering to them by the custodians of common institutions take care only of a small part of the substance of mankind. Drives, precedent in terms of time, causatively ahead, are secondary in terms of value, because the man who really lives, lives directed towards the self which is not yet, the potential to be. Thus, the primacy, the honour, the pride of place in terms of worth or importance goes, in an integrated disciplined society, to those experiencings or states of being which are, or appear to be, in rarity, intermittent, only occasional visitors on the human stage. Rare but galvanising, their power is disproportionate to their spatial extension or temporal duration.

Where is the human soul, self or spirit rooted? Most assuredly in the field of naturalistic forces. But there is this, that this variously named entity (a state of being really) has become independent of its progenitor — i.e., the immediate, circumstantial or material causation and the compulsions endemic to it. Soul is the name for that power of independence, to act, to be, or to endure — on motives which are in seeming diametric opposition to values of personal survival. It apparently, has little care for its place or position in the social or power nexus. This may be deemed obduracy or obstinacy in the face of facts though, from the long-term perspective of human history (or hindsight at least), it is not mere perversity.

Some such model of the human centre must be accepted if we are to proceed any further with our task of erecting a framework of values, to distinguish between primary value and tertiary or the instrumental ones. There must be one universal pattern, before the patterns of society or its multifarious conditions can be profitably talked about or developed.

The human prospect hinges on this: on the realisation that, social institutions, political patterns and ultimately — at base — the model that informs such institutions, etc., must refer back to those psychic elements in the individual who, if he so chooses, can become a person. Social endeavour remains calamitous without this timeless foresight.

What are the forces at play in our world? Control of material and social realities by individuals, by super-systems of individuals — so far so good. And what are individuals? — combinations of beliefs-unbeliefs, conscious reasonings, subconscious, half-articulate thoughts. Thus, in the post-Freud period, it should not be difficult to see, that, the irrational element in human nature still plays a big enough part in the impeccable seeming calculations, promptings, and moves of nations, and efficiently reasoning individuals; of little import then that the public image of Nation States is made to seem so decorous, all sweetness and light. Scientifically speaking even the world's circumstances are not fully in control, less than half so.

I am not suggesting that a whole people or individuals will be full of conscious ill-will; no, but then there is this other paradox, that born to a socio-cultural ethos which is the consequence of Missionary or Marxist zeal for material or structural improvements, from their very melioristic viewpoints people can now have difficulty granting cogence, pride of place to that inner, personal, vertical self which, to my mind, can only be neglected at civilisations' dire peril. Rival institutions of tremendous power, often champions for human good but unwittingly for ill, hold back the energies of the self I postulated in check. Thus, under the present dispensation (of huge concentrated power) it is inevitable that the activities of the deeper self are greatly reduced or buried. They are turned to apathy, passivity or a simple resignation — even as the outward, intellectual man remains alert, active, soberly reasoning. But where the deeper self has gone to sleep or is suppressed, there lurks danger — to its possesser as much as to society. Post-Freud, we know where the danger lies, quite invisible though it may be to workaday eyes.

In even brand new politico-social orders, brought into existence so well meaningly, is yet observed the ground for a pessimistic outlook and much bafflement, for does not the grand progress of this same world end up in much recurring regress, in diabolic unpleasantness, in clannish pettiness, to pure mindlessness, not meaning brainlessness? Yes, sundry pettinesses all, yet these range from putting a few millions to sleep, to denial of shelter to strangers.

Perhaps the old cruelty is still 'human' though of a barbaric style. But what of the civilised unwarlike impersonality, with its absence of common feeling? — is it not a resultant of excessive braininess? — the desire for giganticism — at bottom the simple need of an unformed soul for glory, vanity, condescension, or the cultivation of styles of life which are heavily biased towards the fun and games of outward activities. Here, the self born of mutual sharing, identification and sympathy (or of spiritual union) is only in an incipient condition, not really brought to birth.

A state lacking in individuals with such selves has to it little of the future alternatives or the deeper self-determinations. A society needs power, of all sorts, and of course it needs to share such power and goods, else it comes to grief through sheer lower level conflicts.

But a given society's power (the supreme) is the power of those of its individuals who stand in opposition to collectivity, not perversely, but purely procedurely, like one electric pole to the other; without this no creative charge is produced. The power of spirit (an old fashioned term perhaps, and non-scientifically couched) certainly can be explained in scientific terms, but its true meaning emerges to one only in the process of living in interchange; it can hardly be well conveyed through discursive, propositional language. The power of such spirit must remain constant in any society, and its meaning must repeatedly be clarified and amplified, and their meaning must stand in a central position *vis-a-vis* the equations of power.

I certainly do not mean by the word spirit, the desacrilised intellect; this sophistic mind is not what we are in want of today, nor do I mean by it the functions dispersed by any sort of orthodox or state priesthood. I mean by the worn out expression that working unity of the aesthetic-moral intellect, before whose presence the individual bows down or at least his ego bows down, at the least inwardly. It would certainly therefore, to my way of thinking, not do to desacrilise or denude psychic concepts and meanings, and so on of their patina of intention, feeling and sentiment. The fructifying chemistry of myth must remain as it was or there is spiritual erosion (like there is in the disappearance of vegetation over a bare rock), an end to life-giving celebration over plain fact. And little remains of value. Under these circumstances, human prospects, human future, cannot have much taste, and will only have outward, still more acrimonious, conflicts; and if not those then there will be an atrophy in sympathy of relationships, a fact corroborated by very many novelists and thinkers of the world, directly or else by revealing the lack of emotion or life-interest in their characters, indirectly. The literature of apathy and emptiness is well known. Most of such literature, as also the psychoanalytical case studies, pertain to the 'developed' mankind.

The task for us is that of a reassessment of human development; have we by good intentions, by applying our minds diligently, arrived at a physically elevated position but where yet no true literature is possible and where the grand public rituals have to them little of the sap of life?

The proposition is this: can man retain reasonable self-possession, self assurance, freedom from the cramping twilight of fear, be the master of 'his fate', yet combine it all with an essential imagination engendered humility, a lack of ethnic conceit, lack of self idolatory?

To any culture, mood or attitude are all important; humility, or conceit, which is it to be? — if a civilisation (an amalgam of complicated horizontal and vertical values) retains in its mood a charity towards 'other' races and neighbours, and if it does not overrate its own brilliance and inventiveness to the point of arrogance, culture is right. A modicum of understanding may, here, be possible between humans. In other words conflicts between humans are not merely economic; these are also cultural born, as say, of a Brahmanical pride or a Mandarin aloofness. But a civilisation which has learnt to retain at its core the sympathetic mood of literature (that concentration upon the activities of the human soul in its loves and despairs) has the possibility of essential balance. Such civilisation does not denigrate human intellect or inventive or conceptual cleverness but it does not overvalue it, nor turn it into mere material for power; it has no avarice for unalloyed political privilege. What I have been trying to sell is, what I claim to be the central value for the individual — the queen bee to which all the other 'bees' of values subscribe. It is the image of excellence that different societies and different strata of populations have harboured in their bosoms, and all that matters in the end.

The value or the *perennial pattern par excellence* must be universal, cutting across continents, stemming as it would from the essential human quality, of a human character rooted in imagination which, without being fanatical, still has nerve. Now in a culture, increasingly given to research, analysis, cerebration, often employed on purely state-backed humanitarian causes, the subject almost evaporates. This 'centre' disappears or else it inheres, not in being whole but purely in observing detachedly, noticing uninvolvedly and so on. If a whole society gives itself up to this, somewhat cold bloodedness, it loses an essential focus; it forgets that it is still creature. What has happened is, that, this society has lost itself in excessive calculation of the phenomenal world; it is now, in terms of affect, much too 'outside' of the world, and cannot act from conviction. has no power of decision from deep within. Now the new technological culture, abundantly rich as it is in engineered creativity and fraught with great and good possibilities for the future of mankind, is for the moment, short on one important component (to use the mechanistic terminology). The new society does not seem to know that it also needs the services of that energy within mankind which though not based on scientific reasoning, is none the less the vital heart of man's psyche *qua* man. An energy which, in other words, fatefully effects his behaviour both by acts of omission as of commission; here is a psychosomatically rooted sacred element and not a construct to be ordered into being by fiat. This, so to say seed, needs slow nurture; requires that much allowance be made to it by legislature, law courts, the sovereign. It is veritably the seed of being, one that prospers on awe and wonder, and in turn extracts submission from all who have come under its spell. Its mystery is not open to too much analysis, it representing personal growth and not a measurable quantity. Question is, what is the relationship of the individual to the whole, to an ethos, to the sum and substance of his life, and which this seed represents? Is the relationship only contractual or is it also irrevocable in some essential meaning of that term? The future which I would see realised, for realistic as well idealistic reasons is one in which some sort of sacred is re-established at the heart of the individual and, thus, of the human community.

There is, or ought be, the following aside as one begins to think of that trying matter, of tradition *versus* modernity: that the sacred or the numinous must be secured from its warpings and degenerations in traditional social orders, which rich though they are in feeling, are also iniquitious by virtue of their frequent absent-mindedness towards questions of the just relations between groups, in-between communities, as well as in being weak in the repertoire of rational-empirical thought. The sacred cannot live too securely in company with an inhuman environment or where social conflicts are merely suppressed, where the human personality is merely crushed unaer denials. Scientific modes of thought (which plainly are prosaic realistic modes, began already in the ancient world, though without the new applications) are quite contrary to the ritual modes of human behaviour (verbal or any other); and during the prevalence of only ritual modes little open enquiry had been possible as to nature or human institutions. But enquiry is important even as ritual is. Any fresh reorganisation of institutions and laws based on its results could save the sacred (or feeling) from being perverted in the dark superstitions of the sub-mind which flourishes in a culture of poverty. And yet the 'sacred' must not be confused or mistaken for all these various enlightened processes of today, which are more functional than fateful; the sacred is a life and death concern of self with itself, with all its headaches, of meaning, goal, purpose. Far too many of the outward problems stem from inwards, from the root—they have not been quite so linked, causatively. Any design for living must observe that, too often childish human wishes, even as at times genuine vision, set history into motion, this or that way; that these wishes are the true directors of the human drama; and these secret pathetic, soulless wishes must be inspected closely.

The dichotomies between economic, social, political forces and so on are facts, but these disturbing realities must in turn be examined in the light of the energy expended by society on different personal goals. If a nation has little energy to spare for privacies — to separate things that are Caeser's from those that are not Caeser's and if all of life is made out to be a public question or problem — no alter-ego, alter-self will be left to compare, contrast and test existing values and realities. Truth emerges only via contests, by relative contrasts, or mutual self-questionings by different powers of self. When this is not possible passivity, fanaticism or unrealism result — as seems to be the case today when unbridled economic growth or power becomes the holiest of desires. These only lead to conflict by their very nature, since they stem from material interests, that cannot ever be spiritually productive. Only conflicts on the plane of spirit or ideas can be creative — i.e., if they are not mere facades for material goals. There will have to be radical shifts, in emphasis, on the priorities of social effort, as well as a realisation of the proper goals of political or collective heroism.

The sacred, then, concerns the individual *qua* individual, or that part of him which can commune with his fellows, and share sentiment, but it can do so only through some non-coercive agency, i.e., through insight, sympathy, growth in fraternal feeling and so on. The power delegated to the State cannot bring this about. Here, the State must learn to leave it alone, not cultivate a national church.

I doubt, however, if the states of today will soon learn to shed their paternalisms, the tendency to organise, rationalise, explicate all manner of activity, even if it be most private. Thus, when nothing remains under shadow or shade, nothing of the sort I deem important can ever germinate; and since power, as one knows, has its own logic of destructive conflict, an interference in the secret processes of the human soul is on the cards. The state (or organised power — often in accord with the antediluvian, archaic images and models of the collective self) itself bloats and battens on science: or, rather, on scientific knowhow and quantified proposition and argument, strained of all charge or sense of human emotion and sentiment. Now, therefore, science plays into the hands of the atavistic state; it provides it increasing power to control and to coerce the natural environment and also the human constituents; sometimes for the benefit of the latter, also, often, in the course of chasing towards overpowering abstractions and promptings. These, which issue out of that amalgam — the nationality — which is history, culture whatever else, as well as organised self-interest. Of these, culture is more open to corruption, insanity and the inertia of habit. There, moreover, is also the logic of power itself—like water it is bound to find its own way, which may be destructive of all fragile experiences.

What I see is, that, for peace in the heart (and so in the future) to be lasting, it has to be derived from age old, if renewed, renovated sentiments, images, symbols; they must capture the mind of the world community, must cut across all kind of boundaries — religious or any other. There will be conflict of sentiments, of the broader and the narrower. There is also this added difficulty, that to the traditional or old, the new seems all mundane because the sacred in it is not recognised, simply because it is in the contemporary grab. This calls for imagination.

All the same, one can foresee that all kinds of creeds, racial groups and other natural or unnatural divisions will, with the growth and evolution of mind, and through contact and familiarity, but also by conscious reflection, undergo a slow but steady transformation; one can foresee too that with knowledge of self, of literature and of other arts, religions and the so-called races cannot be as sectarian as of old. Changes are indeed already afoot; a kind of liberalism, pliability or flexibility to moral vision is bound to arrive. Given inner knowledge a set of firmer sentiments come into play — these which have synthesised normative realities within the nexus of the new but plain natural facts.

What I must, at this point is that single out the so-called aesthetic and creative values, as expressed in the guidelines, do not follow (in time) after man's fundamental needs (whatever these might be) are satisfied; so one must not say that 'one hopes these will also be given attention'. This division of needs and functions, from the creative or aesthetic energies has in fact been fatal to civilisation creating a schizophrenic split. The creative, or any other dimension, must form one seamless whole, or the total condition comes to grief. The man of any time, especially so of today, needs a creative attitude to the functional to keep his spirit whole; the matter is one of style, and style is what matters. Most values are the children of the creative imagination, whether these pertain to morals or to the marketplace. Even seemingly more mundane things cannot exist one at the cost of the other, in separation. Skills must not be reduced to the purely functional or the decorative — nor be vetted and sundered from life values; this way they cannot have much meaning, cogency or power.

The quality of man's life? — it has only partly to do with a kingdom of things, important as they are, but rather more to do with arrangements between things and thoughts, between behaviour and self-images. Which images are we furthering? Do these lead to growth of self, or conflict between self and the self of the community? It appears there has been a breakdown of such understanding between self and community, and vacuum between communities. It is not merely a question of satisfying man's basic needs at once — unless at times of famine and war — but of satisfying them how. Man lives and satisfies his needs through multiple levels of being, and not in isolation and piecemeal; it is great simplification to plan from the outside, or from up top, the human good.

Values, related as they are to meaning, arise out of reflection; out of guiding the course of one's life in the light of considered ends. Such consideration certainly entails a gap in time, between desire and fulfilment, the very name for civilisation.

Now there is this paradox — in nature or historical time — that the great mental revolutions, which have transformed man's outer environments and also inner understandings, have not fully brought to a higher point of perfection the refinement in his motivations — I would not say emotions; poverty of culture is what will kill man as much as lack of bread — by self-disgust, or by contempt towards his neighbour. The revolution must go deeper; it must attempt to articulate, in metaphor or through meditation, and forms of art or craft, the self-surpassing spirit of man. The insights of seers and thinkers have been neglected; they can do much to rescue the individual from oblivion or self-contempt. Self-values are not created by taking thought alone, but by immersing in processes of living. Values are certainly clarified and preserved by critical thought; critical thought however must not usurp the place of the values themselves; values such as I have in mind exact sanctity, whereas on the other hand scientific thought demands rather more of a deference or patient hearing. But, in this context, any thought which has become tool is distinct from the inner nature of poetic metaphor, religious mass, visual image, and the live gestures or customs which are designed to provide intrinsic satisfaction and strength.

That must be the essential pattern, if human prospects are to be such as ensure dignity for mankind. But a variety of patterns such an overall total pattern must guarantee — for instance in the ensuring of the unexpected, which is the name for creativity. It must ensure difference, choice, idiosyncrasy, in the proliferation and the extension of values, in the experiences of worth, in the variations and the richness of human existences. Any social order or social ideology must make room for this search into patterns no matter if they are formed of the same essential constituents.

But the dynamic pattern which allows these differences, must remain fixed, as the fundamental premise. This itself must not be called into question; or else chaos, anarchy, the closed society are in prospect on the horizon.

What of traditional values today? If affirmation of these means unrevised belief then one must say no to them. But modern science — as enquiry — as I already said is, as we know, itself not so modern, being refined common sense it is/perennial; what we must ensure is that the tradition of enquiry must be made safe through the agencies of law and legislature — enquiry into nature and human fact and event. But, I repeat, enquiry is one facet of man's soul, the others are experiencing; the becoming and being, through experience of value, of self-surpassing, imaginative or actual psychic encounters. Are these last traditional attitudes? Yes and no; our job is to ensure a full creative tradition; the tradition that renews itself, even the tradition of science for science is not without shadows, is not omniscient or omnipresent. However, a combination or 'religion' and science is a fruitless occupation; what is needed is a redefinition, in contemporary terms, of the integrating experience which is emotional and so on rather than in merely being in conflict with the work or findings of science or objective method. Most religious people today are outside the fold of organised religions, and to say that they are merely ethical will not quite do; their experience of value, their passions as perhaps their morals pertain to and are born in an awareness of the totality of world or life experience, and not merely in response to a limited social life.

A good bit of what I have prescribed pertains to long-term goals — which are not within the fulfilment of a lifetime. But that is why these are termed religious or teleological, the *telos* that man projects into the future, to give his immediate life more meaning and direction than those given to dumb and deaf creatures. The long term is likely to be ignored because it is easily forgotten. But then man is the memory binder; living in and out of time he lives by incentives which are not sensory, not immediate, not present; he relates himself to goals — whether sane or insane which are 'other-worldly' so to speak. Man is not a creature of time alone; a purely practical society catering to common needs and so on is likely to be a limited one and a failure even as the old ones were, living pathologically in reveries and fantasy; it will be so because man's true nature demands vision but which is the channel denied to him too often.

Under the given scheme of things, placed at the very heart of the causal, physical processes, born of them, a creature of them, as of the subsequently developed institutions and historical accidents, humankind has, as we know, by virtue of a cortical development, luck, chance, and choice become independent to an extent — a factor to reckon with, in his own unfolding. His conscience and consciousness are born of his reaction to and reflection on environments. Thus, ideas and ideation, and no matter in what forms these come, become his most vital mental property, levers for readjusting or readapting to his physical circumstance or social behaviour. Human future then is linked to seminal ideas, and as to their force in synthesising or unifying disparate, contradictory and wasteful activities. Ideas are in turn the result of the will to freedom (not freedom from life), the struggle on a transmuted cultural plane of the struggle for survival. Purely technological devices or blue prints are only the pale shadows of such ideas; ideas have a content — and the most important of them are of a personal meaning, and which in turn entails fateful involvement. Both the personal and the impersonal are equally fused in the total dynamics. The man of the future will have to recombine in himself both the inward and the outward vision, both self-distrust and self-command.

Man, as we can well imagine, has been a slave for a good part of his existence in one or other meanings of that term. Man is free in some senses today, and he is not really a slave to metallic or other machines, only an addict; but then he can be found to be a slave to machines of organisations and gigantic institutions – there is the crux, the root of the helplessness, of the barrenness or poverty of being, of the difficulty of achieving a humane soul. But with ideas which guide the spirit and which in turn guides action, there is a slim possibility of partial salvation, collectively or at least individually.

List of Contributors

Baidyanath Saraswati	Anthropologist Indira Gandhi National Centre for the Arts Janpath New Delhi
M.C. Joshi	Archaeologist Indira Gandhi National Centre for the Arts Janpath New Delhi
Prema Nandakumar	Spiritualist Mudal Tirumaligai 91, South Chitra Street Srirangam
Prem Lata Sharma	Musicologist Banaras Hindu University Varanasi
Raghava R. Menon	Musicologist M-14, Greater Kailash-I New Delhi
Sitakant Mahapatra	Anthropologist 21 Satyanagar Bhubaneswar

Ramesh Chandra Shah	Poet Professor Colony Vidya Vihar Bhopal
S.C. Malik	Anthropologist 185 Mandakini Enclave New Delhi
M.M. Agarwal	Philosopher 21-B, Dilshad Garden Delhi
Alok Rai	Social Scientist Indian Institute of Technology New Delhi
Ashok R. Kelkar	Linguist 7, Dhananjay Pune
Keshav Malik	Poet 5/90, Connaught Circus New Delhi

Index